THE WORLD'S H🔥T SPOTS

Saudi Arabia

Adrian Sinkler, *Book Editor*

Daniel Leone, *President*
Bonnie Szumski, *Publisher*
Scott Barbour, *Managing Editor*

GREENHAVEN
PRESS ®

THOMSON
GALE

San Diego • Detroit • New York • San Francisco • Cleveland
New Haven, Conn. • Waterville, Maine • London • Munich

© 2003 by Greenhaven Press. Greenhaven Press is an imprint of The Gale Group, Inc., a division of Thomson Learning, Inc.

Greenhaven® and Thomson Learning™ are trademarks used herein under license.

For more information, contact
Greenhaven Press
27500 Drake Rd.
Farmington Hills, MI 48331-3535
Or you can visit our Internet site at http://www.gale.com

Cover credit: © Associated Press, Pool

LIBRARY OF CONGRESS CATALOGING-IN-PUBLICATION DATA

Saudi Arabia / Adrian Sinkler, book editor.
 p. cm. — (The world's hot spots)
Includes bibliographical references and index.
ISBN 0-7377-1812-9 (pbk. : alk. paper) — ISBN 0-7377-1811-0 (lib. : alk. paper)
 1. United States—Foreign relations—Saudi Arabia. 2. Saudi Arabia—Foreign relations—United States. 3. United States—Foreign relations—2001– .
4. September 11 Terrorist Attacks, 2001. I. Sinkler, Adrian. II. Series.
E183.8.S25 S28 2003
327.730538—dc21   2002192535

Printed in the United States of America

🔥 CONTENTS

Chapter 1: The Historical Roots of Saudi Arabia's Current Tensions

1. Wahhabi Islam and the Rise of the Al Saud Monarchy

In the mid-eighteenth century, an Arabian prince and a
conservative religious leader joined forces and began a
quest to conquer the Arabian Peninsula that was not
fully realized until 1932.

2. The Birth of Saudi Arabia

With the help of the British government, the founder of
the modern kingdom of Saudi Arabia successfully completed a thirty-year process of political unification on the
Arabian Peninsula.

3. The Discovery of Oil and Social Change in Saudi Arabia

The interior of the Arabian Peninsula remained isolated
from the outside world until the discovery of oil in 1937,
which dramatically changed the way the nomadic
Bedouin of Saudi Arabia lived and interacted with their
political and economic systems.

4. Difficult Changes in Saudi Arabia After the Gulf War

Iraq's invasion of Kuwait in August 1990 forced the
Saudi monarchy to make some difficult choices, including the decision to station over 500,000 American troops
in Saudi Arabia that created a rift between conservative
Muslims and liberal business and political leaders.

Chapter 2: Saudi Arabia and the September 11, 2001, Attacks on America

Chapter 3: Tensions and Changes in Saudi Arabian Foreign Relations

the United States and to the rest of the Middle East, but it is not in the interest of American policy makers to press for a change in Saudi behavior.

2. An Argument for the Expulsion of American Forces from Saudi Arabia

by Hayder Ali Khan

Criticism of the Saudi alliance with the United States reached a crescendo after September 11, 2001, as Muslims throughout the Arab world clamored for the removal of American bases from Saudi Arabia.

3. A Saudi-Iranian Rapprochement Is Harmful to American Interests

by Martin Sieff

After years of being at odds, Saudi Arabia and Iran improved their relationship in the latter half of the 1990s, reaching agreements on issues such as oil prices and the Israeli-Palestinian conflict and creating potential problems for America's Middle East policy.

4. A Saudi Plan for Peace Between Israel and the Palestinians

by Abdullah Ibn Abdul Aziz Al Saud

The Saudi government demonstrated a change in its approach to the Arab-Israeli conflict in the Middle East when it became directly involved in the process to reach a peace settlement between the Israelis and the Palestinians in early 2002.

5. The West Should Dismantle the Al Saud Monarchy

by Mark Steyn

Its support for radical Islamic movements makes Saudi Arabia an unreliable ally and leaves Western leaders with no other choice than to forcefully remove the Al Saud from power.

Chapter 4: The Prospects for Reform in Saudi Arabia

1. Saudi Economic and Social Reform Will Come Slowly

by Eric Rouleau

Due to conservative elements within the Saudi leader-

ship, rapid liberalization of the nation's social policies
and political system is unlikely.

2. The Al Saud Dynasty Will Remain in Power
by Bill Powell
Its oil wealth and its unique political system will enhance the ability of Saudi Arabia's monarchy to resist
internal opposition and to remain in power for the fore-
seeable future.

3. Saudi Arabia Commits Human Rights Abuses
by Human Rights Watch
The Saudi Arabian government continues to abuse the
rights of its citizens in various ways, such as forbidding
the formation of political parties, falsely imprisoning
and torturing suspected opponents, and denying women
basic educational and employment opportunities.

4. Christians Must Promote Religious Freedom in Saudi Arabia
by Jeff M. Sellers
Christians must act to end the persecution and intolerance wrought by the religious authorities in Saudi
Arabia.

5. Saudi Arabia Is Committed to the Cause of Universal Human Rights
by Torki Mohammed Saud Al-Kabeer
In spite of international criticism, Saudi Arabia remains
committed to human rights and is taking steps to ensure
that it honors international treaties without neglecting its
Islamic heritage.

♦ FOREWORD

The American Heritage Dictionary defines the term *hot spot* as "an area in which there is dangerous unrest or hostile action." Though it is probably true that almost any conceivable "area" contains potentially "dangerous unrest or hostile action," there are certain countries in the world especially susceptible to conflict that threatens the lives of noncombatants on a regular basis. After the events of September 11, 2001, the consequences of this particular kind of conflict and the importance of the countries, regions, or groups that produce it are even more relevant for all concerned public policy makers, citizens, and students. Perhaps now more than ever, the violence and instability that engulfs the world's hot spots truly has a global reach and demands the attention of the entire international community.

The scope of problems caused by regional conflicts is evident in the extent to which international policy makers have begun to assert themselves in efforts to reduce the tension and violence that threatens innocent lives around the globe. The U.S. Congress, for example, recently addressed the issue of economic stability in Pakistan by considering a trading bill to encourage growth in the Pakistani textile industry. The efforts of some congresspeople to improve the economic conditions in Pakistan through trade with the United States was more than an effort to address a potential economic cause of the instability engulfing Pakistani society. It was also an acknowledgment that domestic issues in Pakistan are connected to domestic political issues in the United States. Without a concerted effort by policy makers in the United States, or any other country for that matter, it is quite possible that the violence and instability that shatters the lives of Pakistanis will not only continue, but will also worsen and threaten the stability and prosperity of other regions.

Recent international efforts to reach a peaceful settlement of the Israeli-Palestinian conflict also demonstrate how peace and stability in the Middle East is not just a regional issue. The toll on Palestinian and Israeli lives is easy to see through the suicide bombings and rocket attacks in Israeli cities and in the occupied territories of the West Bank and Gaza. What is, perhaps, not as evident is the extent to which this conflict involves the rest of the world. Saudi Arabia and Iran, for instance, have long been at odds and have attempted to gain control of the conflict by supporting competing organizations dedicated to a Palestinian state. These groups have often used Saudi and Iranian financial and political support to carry out violent attacks against Israeli civilians and military installations. Of course, the issue goes far beyond a struggle between two regional powers to gain control of the region's most visible issue. Many analysts and leaders have also argued that the West's military and political support of Israel is one of the leading factors that motivated al-Qaeda's September 11 attacks on New York and Washington, D.C. In many ways, this regional conflict is an international affair that will require international solutions.

The World's Hot Spots series is intended to meet the demand for information and discussion among young adults and students who would like to better understand the areas embroiled in conflicts that contribute to catastrophic events like those of September 11. Each volume of The World's Hot Spots is an anthology of primary and secondary documents that provides historical background to the conflict, or conflicts, under examination. The books also provide students with a wide range of opinions from world leaders, activists, and professional writers concerning the root causes and potential solutions to the problems facing the countries covered in this series. In addition, extensive research tools such as an annotated table of contents, bibliography, and glossaries of terms and important figures provide readers a foundation from which they can build their knowledge of some of the world's most pressing issues. The information and opinions presented in The World's Hot Spots series will give students some of the tools they will need to become active participants in the ongoing dialogue concerning the globe's most volatile regions.

🔥 INTRODUCTION

The Conflict Between Tradition and Change in Saudi Arabia

During the last several decades of the twentieth century, Saudi Arabia emerged as one of the most strategically and economically important countries in the world. The discovery of large oil reserves on the Arabian Peninsula during the 1930s led many world leaders to the conclusion that Saudi Arabia was vital to their national interests. Access to affordable energy resources, which Saudi Arabia helped provide for much of the twentieth century, became tremendously important for industrial and postindustrial economies in Europe, North America, and Asia. But to nearly 1 billion Muslims around the world, Saudi Arabia remains significant not because of its oil wealth but because it contains the two holiest sites in Islam, the cities of Mecca and Medina. Each year, nearly 2 million hajjis, or pilgrims, from every country on Earth travel to Saudi Arabia and visit the holy shrines located in these two cities.

Saudi political leaders have attempted to balance their strategic and economic importance in international politics with their position as guardians of Islam's two holiest sites since the country's founding, but it has not always been an easy task. On one hand, the Saudi royal family has relied on its adherence to a conservative Islamic doctrine for domestic support from a largely conservative population. This emphasis on conservative Islamic traditions has encouraged the growth of fundamentalist groups that advocate a return to ways of life that predate the creation of modern Saudi Arabia. On the other hand, the royal family has also relied on Western technologies, ideas, and armies for its wealth and for protection from external enemies. This exposure to foreign influences has simultaneously encouraged the growth of groups oriented toward reforming Saudi political and religious institutions according to Western models. Though there are many historical themes that emerge in this volume, the most common is this conflict between Saudi religious traditions and change initiated through contact with Western technologies and belief systems.

Needless to say, this conflict has always produced significant challenges for Saudi political leaders and their allies, but during the late twentieth and early twenty-first centuries, the challenges grew in intensity and involved more than just Saudi Arabians. The most visible expression of how intense these challenges had become and how far they had spread came on September 11, 2001, when fifteen Saudi citizens helped orchestrate terrorist attacks on the World Trade Center in New York and the Pentagon in Washington, D.C. In the months following the attacks, Saudi political leaders came under increased pressure from every imaginable source to reform their political system and to rearrange their international alliances. In its most extreme forms, this pressure was aimed at dismantling the existing Saudi political system and replacing it with a conservative Islamic theocracy.

But the challenges Saudi leaders face, though they grew in intensity and scope, did not begin on September 11, 2001. Instead, they are the result of a broader historical landscape that shaped and influenced the world inherited by contemporary leaders from previous generations. The eighteenth-century social scientist Karl Marx perhaps said it best in his *Eighteenth Brumaire of Louis Bonaparte* when he noted that "men make their own history . . . but under circumstances directly found, given and transmitted from the past." As is true for every country around the world, the challenges that currently face Saudi Arabia are inextricably linked to its own historical development.

The Significance of Islam in the Kingdom of Saudi Arabia

The history of Saudi Arabia is tightly interwoven with the development of Islam, which began over eleven hundred years before the establishment of the first Saudi state at the end of the eighteenth century. The prophet Muhammad was born in the city of Mecca, which is located in the central-western Saudi province of Hejaz, and began his career just north of his birthplace in about A.D. 610. Muhammad eventually fled Mecca to avoid persecution, setting up a theocratic state based on his teachings in Medina ("City of the Prophet") from which he managed to conquer most of Arabia and convert much of the population to the religion of Islam. After his death in 632, several rifts developed between Islamic leaders concerning who would succeed the prophet as the earthly king of Muslims. Though these rifts have never fully closed, all Muslims still look on the cities of Mecca and Medina as two of the holiest sites in the Islamic religion. The fact that Saudi Arabia contains these two cities gives it a special significance in the Muslim world, evidenced by the fact that Saudi's King Fahd refers to himself as "the custodian of the two holy mosques."

However, the process through which the modern Kingdom of Saudi Arabia came to control the two holiest sites in Islam did not begin until the mid–eighteenth century and would not end until 1932. The long and protracted struggle to unify a region characterized by many historians and ethnographers as a highly fragmented and nomadic society was both turbulent and violent. Ultimately, the unification of the Arabian Peninsula depended on an alliance between the prince of a small village and a conservative Islamic reform movement known in the Western world as Wahhabism.

Religious Revival in Eighteenth-Century Arabia

In 1740 the man for which the Wahhabi movement is named, Sheikh Muhammad ibn Abd al-Wahhab, began an aggressive attempt to reform the religious practices of Muslims on the Arabian Peninsula because of what he perceived to be a dangerous relapse into pre-Islamic practices. The practice that most pained Wahhab was the tendency of Muslims to revert to a form of polytheism, or the worship of multiple gods and saints, which he deemed contrary to the teachings of the prophet Muhammad. Facing heavy resistance from the establishment *ulama* (religious scholars), Wahhab began proselytizing a strict interpretation of Islamic law that was based on a literal reading of the Koran and hadith, or the teachings and writings of Muhammad.

The central characteristics of Wahhab's doctrine were its insistence on a literal adherence to *shariah* (Islamic law) and its aggressive stance toward *Bid'a* (religious innovation). Any and all forms of religious practice not explicitly endorsed in the *shariah* were deemed un-Islamic, and those who practiced them were subject to jihad (holy war) by Wahhab and his adherents. Wahhabism also called for the abolishment of all forms of ostentatious worship, including a ban on music, and stressed an austere existence that consisted solely of the worship of God. Wahhab's movement rapidly gained followers, but it also faced continuous pressure from other religious and tribal leaders on the Arabian Peninsula, which remained extremely fragmented politically during the eighteenth century. In order to resist those who sought to destroy his movement to reform Islam in Arabia, Wahhab made an alliance with the ruler of Dar'iya, a small city in the central Arabian province of Najd.

The ruler's name was Muhammad Ibn Saud, and he loosely controlled a small and relatively insignificant tribal confederation of Bedouin warriors in the area surrounding his village. Ibn Saud agreed to allow the sheikh to control religious affairs in his small kingdom largely because it bolstered his support among the local population and gave him access to much-needed resources in the form of a religious tax called the *zakat*. The alliance also gave the prince a religious justification to expand his control beyond the confines of his small village and to reform the religious practices of neighboring Arabian kingdoms. Though it had relatively humble beginnings, the alliance between Ibn Saud and the sheikh would soon become a formidable force on the Arabian Peninsula.

Protected from his enemies near his home of al-Uyaynah, Wahhab increased his following and with the aid of Ibn Saud began his jihad against the religious innovators that he felt were threatening the purity of Islam. By the early nineteenth century, the descendants of Ibn Saud and Wahhab extended their influence over much of northern and central Arabia, including both Mecca and Medina by the end of 1806. The expansion of Saudi-Wahhabi control of the Arabian Peninsula proved to be short-lived, however, ending with the Ottoman-Egyptian invasion and evacuation of Arabia in 1811. The alliance would continue in a weaker form for the remainder of the nineteenth century, confined mostly to the area surrounding Riyadh, which is the modern capital of Saudi Arabia. Due to internal warfare among the descendants of Ibn Saud, the family was unable to achieve the level of influence it had gained earlier in the century, but it would not be long until the Saudi-Wahhabi alliance reached the zenith of its power and influence.

The Emergence of a Modern Theocracy in Saudi Arabia

The founder of modern Saudi Arabia, Abd al-Aziz ibn Abd ar-Rahman Al Saud (hereafter Ibn Saud), began a thirty-year struggle to reassert Saudi hegemony over the Arabian Peninsula during the winter of 1902, and he would not have succeeded were it not for a combination of factors. Not the least important of these factors was the support of the Wahhabi *ulama* in his home province of Najd. Re-

gaining the allegiance of the Wahhabi establishment was not a given, even though the Al Saud family shared historical ties with the descendants of Wahhab. In fact, several *ulama* in the city of Riyadh initially professed their allegiance to the Rashidi dynasty, which was in control of the city at the time of Ibn Saud's invasion. The *ulama* of Riyadh only offered their allegiance to Ibn Saud after he had secured control of the city in February 1902.

Once Ibn Saud obtained the allegiance of the *ulama* of Riyadh and the neighboring city of Qasim—a process that took several years— he also inherited the support of a group of Wahhabi religious scholars known as the *mutawwa*. Not only were they schooled in and deeply committed to the conservative religious doctrines of Wahhab, but they also formed and instructed a religious military corps called the *Ikhwan*. Composed of nomadic Bedouins, the *Ikhwan* became an important force in Ibn Saud's army and were ultimately instrumental in expanding and consolidating his control of the Arabian Peninsula. Of course, the allegiance of the *Ikhwan* to Ibn Saud existed only as long as he had the support of the Wahhabi religious establishment, and as long as he remained devoted to jihad against religious innovation in Arabia. There were times when this support was shaken, but for the most part Ibn Saud gained and maintained control of a large and inspired army of religious warriors.

The renewal of the Saudi-Wahhabi alliance in the first decades of the twentieth century, in conjunction with the support Ibn Saud received from the British in the years following World War I, proved to be a turning point in the history of the Arabian Peninsula. For the first time, there was a political and military leader both strong and shrewd enough to unify the peninsula under the authority of a single imam (religious king). Ibn Saud proved adept at forming key alliances and at commanding a desert army, both of which were necessary skills given the fragmented political conditions and the harsh climate of the Arabian Peninsula. More importantly, he also proved to be a charismatic and religiously devout leader who was capable of mobilizing a large army committed to the unification of Arabia and the reform of its religious institutions.

The Saudi-Wahhabi forces eventually gained control of the Hejaz, including the cities of Mecca and Medina, in 1926. Distrust among the Wahhabi *ulama* and *Ikhwan* made it difficult for Ibn Saud to consolidate his control of the peninsula after his conquest of the Hejaz. Many within the religious establishment feared that Ibn Saud's alliance with the British, his introduction of new technologies, such as the telegraph, and his refusal to continue the war of conquest beyond the borders of Saudi Arabia, indicated only a lukewarm commitment to religious principles.

Eventually, with the aid of important Wahhabi *ulama* in Riyadh, and with the aid of the British air force, Ibn Saud put down resistance to his authority and established the Kingdom of Saudi Arabia, with himself as its king, in September 1932. However, as the period between 1927 and 1930 demonstrated, it was crucial for Ibn Saud to retain his commitment to the revival of Wahhabi religious practices if he wished to maintain control of the kingdom. For this reason, Ibn Saud was careful to maintain a balance of power, much like that of his forebears in the eighteenth century, with the Wahhabi *ulama* in his new domain.

Tensions Between Religious Principles and Political Goals in Saudi Arabia

The banner of Wahhabi Islam gave Ibn Saud a rallying cry to unite groups that once considered themselves autonomous as well as a source of support that bolstered his claims to be king of a unified Arabian Peninsula. Even the Saudi national flag depicts the regime's nominal commitment to Islam with a sword that symbolizes jihad and a slogan in Arabic that reads; "There is no God but Allah, and Muhammad is His Messenger." Indeed, Saudi Arabia's destiny was closely wedded to the region's Islamic heritage from its creation, and its continued survival has, in part, depended on the delicate balance between religious principles and the pragmatic political goals of its rulers.

In order to maintain this balance, Ibn Saud initially ceded a substantial amount of control over matters of state to the Wahhabi *ulama*. For example, he incorporated them into his new administrative system by creating the Committees for Commanding the Good and Forbidding Evil. These committees, officially established in each province during the late 1920s and early 1930s, were given an extensive amount of control over the daily lives of Saudi citizens. The directors and enforcers, who took the name *mutawaa'in* (plural of *mutawwa*), policed public places to ensure that Saudi citizens were not engaging in un-Islamic activity, such as smoking tobacco, drinking alcohol, or mingling with members of the opposite sex. The committees also had the power to arrest violators of Wahhabi principles and to punish them according to prescriptions in the *shariah*, which included the practice of stoning to death those convicted of the most serious crimes.

In exchange for control over the religious purity of the population, the Wahhabi *ulama* sanctioned the rule of Ibn Saud and his sons, providing them with the necessary credentials to command the allegiance of a conservative Islamic society. During the conquest of Arabia, and during the first few years of Ibn Saud's reign, there were some serious conflicts between the religious and political authorities that threatened to upset this power-sharing arrangement. In spite of these conflicts, Ibn Saud was able to maintain control using his acute diplomatic skills, in large part because Arabian society remained relatively unchanged and isolated from foreign influences in the first three decades of the twentieth century. As a result, Ibn Saud's political goals did not frequently come into conflict with those of religious leaders during the early years of his reign. But as international political conditions changed, outside forces made a significant impact on Saudi society and upset the balance between religious principles and the practical concerns of political leaders.

The most significant change in Saudi society began in 1937, when a team of American engineers discovered large oil reserves on the Arabian Peninsula. Ibn Saud gave Standard Oil Company of California (SOCAL) a concession to explore for oil in 1933 because his family needed revenue to pay back debts it incurred during his wars of expansion. The concessions did eventually allow Ibn Saud to pay off his external debts (though they soon mounted again during the late 1940s), but more importantly, SOCAL's exploration of the Arabian Peninsula set in motion a process that gradually brought the Saudi population into contact with Western technologies and belief systems.

The onset of World War II slowed this process, but by the end of the war the foundation had been laid for an oil boom that would rapidly transform Saudi society during the 1950s and 1960s. In 1944 SOCAL and the Saudi government formed the Arabian American Oil Company (ARAMCO), and the U.S. government, through contacts in ARAMCO, began to take an active interest in the internal politics of Saudi Arabia. In order to facilitate the oil exploration and production process, thousands of American and non-Saudi Arabs were brought in to work in the new oil fields. In addition, Western forms of education and administration were introduced to accommodate the growing need for technical knowledge and labor in a modernizing economy. Within two decades, Saudi Arabia transformed from an underdeveloped, nomadic society into a rapidly urbanizing and wealthy country with seemingly unlimited potential for growth. As time passed, these changes also galvanized tensions between conservative Islamic groups and those committed to the transformation of the Saudi political system.

The Rule of King Faisal and the Resurgence of Islamic Principles

After the death of Ibn Saud in 1953, the transformation brought on by advances in the oil industry produced serious strains in Saudi society and in the royal family. Without Ibn Saud's charismatic personality to hold it together, factions within the royal family competed bitterly over issues of succession and the direction of the kingdom's foreign and domestic policies. Ibn Saud's two eldest sons, Saud and Faisal, became embroiled in a conflict that almost tore the royal family apart during the 1950s and early 1960s. Saud initially won the upper hand in the conflict and ascended the Saudi throne in 1953, but his rule was marred by allegations of incompetence and corruption, allowing Faisal to gain the support necessary to replace his brother as king in 1964.

Against the backdrop of conflict within the royal family, a new generation of Saudis developed expectations they obtained from studying abroad and from several key political developments in the

Arab world. The Palestinian-Israeli War of 1948, the Suez Crisis of 1956, and the Six-Day War of 1967 all pitted the Arab nations of the Middle East against the newly formed state of Israel and its Western allies. These developments radicalized several factions within the royal family and within Saudi society as a whole, increasing the prominence of new ideologies that competed with Wahhabi religious doctrine. Though the number of Saudis advocating new ideological orientations and changes in the Saudi government were initially small, their number gradually grew during the 1960s and the early 1970s. Coupled with the royal family's efforts to generate more revenue from the oil industry, which meant encouraging the growth of new technologies and forms of education, these changes reduced the power and influence of the religious establishment.

After ascending the throne in 1964, King Faisal sought to reverse this trend by reasserting his family's historical alliance with the *ulama* and the common Islamic heritage of his Arab neighbors in the Middle East. Faisal increased the role of the *ulama* in the Saudi judicial system and began a campaign to brutally repress political dissidents that called for reforms in the Saudi political system. Faisal also oversaw the transfer of ARAMCO from American to Saudi control and briefly distanced his foreign policy from that of the United States. The weakening of ties with the United States was especially evident during the oil embargo of 1973, during which Saudi Arabia cut off oil supplies to an historical ally. This action was intended to punish the United States for supporting Israel in the Arab-Israeli War of 1973 and to demonstrate to the rest of the Middle East that Saudi Arabia was not a pawn of an imperialist power.

Faisal's policies briefly restored Saudi Arabia's image in the Arab world as a guardian of the sanctity of Islam and demonstrated that, as a result of its oil wealth, Saudi Arabia could be a major player in world politics. However, the Islamic rhetoric and policies of Faisal eventually gave way to practical political concerns. Revolutionary regimes in neighboring countries, such as Syria, Iraq, and South Yemen, continued to challenge the Al Saud family's Islamic credentials because of its historic alliance with the United States. Due to its underdeveloped military complex, the Saudi government was forced to turn to the West to reduce a significant security threat from other Arab countries in the Middle East.

In addition, Saudi Arabia lacked a sufficient number of technical experts necessary for the continued expansion of the oil industry. Without outside aid, the royal family was unable to increase the development of roads and communications technology needed for a modern industrial economy. To make up for these deficiencies, Faisal reestablished close military and technical ties with the United States almost as quickly as he had broken them. A close relationship with the United States was too important to Faisal's political goals to abandon, as it provided him with two important resources: a foil against aggressive neighbors dissatisfied with Saudi Arabia's foreign policy and the technical knowledge and modern equipment needed for a growing oil industry.

Internal Opposition to the Al Saud Monarchy

The reign of Faisal, which ended with his assassination in 1975, threw into stark relief two competing tendencies within Saudi society. On the one hand, Saudi Arabia was a conservative Islamic country that controlled the holy sites of Mecca and Medina, two cities that thousands of Muslims visit during the hajj, or pilgrimage, each year. On the other hand, it was a rapidly changing society that faced enormous internal and external pressure to open up to foreign technology and ideas. Faisal was relatively successful at balancing these two tendencies, both through the repression of dissent and diplomacy, as long as oil revenues continued to climb. Unfortunately for the royal family, oil revenues did not continue to climb, and Faisal's compromise between Islamic ideals and pragmatic political goals began to unravel during the late 1970s.

The most notable manifestation of discontent with the Saudi government came in 1979 when an Islamic opposition group headed by Jhaiman al-Utaibi seized the sacred mosque in Mecca. The group charged the royal family with stealing money from oil revenues that rightfully belonged to the Saudi people and of deviating from Islamic principles, pointing to its dependence on Western countries as evidence. With the aid of French special forces, the Saudi government forced the rebel group out of the mosque and restored order after a two-week confrontation, but the event exposed just how vulnerable the Saudi monarchy was to internal dissent.

During the reigns of King Khalid (1975–1982) and King Fahd (1982–present), the royal family attempted to restore its credibility with Islamic groups by providing large sums to Islamic universities, in spite of shrinking oil revenues, and granting the *mutawaa'in* more power to police the Saudi population. The regime simultaneously placed stringent restrictions on the entry of foreigners and increased the repression of reform-minded dissidents throughout the 1980s. Meanwhile, thousands of Saudi citizens went to fight in Afghanistan, with the support of the Saudi government, in order to aid their fellow

Muslims in a campaign to repel the Soviet army, which invaded its central Asian neighbor in 1979. Throughout the 1980s, Saudi society experienced an Islamic revival that the royal family fully endorsed. However, the Al Saud still retained close ties to the United States in order to counter potential external threats from the Soviet Union and a new revolutionary government in Iran.

The Islamic revival of the 1980s also coincided with a sharp decline in oil revenues that left much of the Saudi population destitute compared to the wealthy and extravagant lifestyle of the royal family. Coupled with increased levels of repression, the growing disparity in wealth between the royal family and the rest of the population contributed to a rise in popular discontent with the Saudi regime. Opposition groups of many different ideological persuasions began to form and press the Saudi government for reforms in both the economy and the political system.

By the end of the 1980s, the Afghan-Soviet War ended, and thousands of mujahideen (religious warriors) returned from Afghanistan to find their country in disarray and their political leaders unwilling, or unable, to correct the economic problems plaguing Saudi Arabia. Many of these young warriors were radicalized by their experience in Afghanistan and returned to their home country determined to challenge the authority of the Al Saud family as well as its commitment to Arabia's Islamic heritage. All of these developments created the fertile soil for the dissent and resistance to the Saudi monarchy that would not only threaten to destabilize Saudi Arabia in the 1990s but would also contribute to the development of one of the world's most notorious terrorist organizations.

The Gulf War, Islamic Fundamentalism, and International Terrorism

Tensions between the political goals of the Saudi monarchy and its commitment to Islamic principles reached a full boil during the early 1990s when two of its closest neighbors went to war. On August 2, 1990, Saddam Hussein's Iraqi army invaded the neighboring country of Kuwait and unleashed a chain of events that transformed the political landscape of the Middle East. Threats from hostile Arab regimes were not anything new for the Saudi monarchy, but Hussein's invasion of Kuwait was the first time a potential enemy became militarily active on the Saudi border. Like many of his predecessors, King Fahd was forced to compromise his commitment to Islamic principles in order to promote his political goals—this time the goal was protection from foreign invasion.

Days after the Iraqi invasion of Kuwait, King Fahd announced he would accept assistance from the United States and allow an international contingent of troops to establish bases on Saudi soil. By January 1991, over 500,000 foreign troops—the vast majority of them American—were stationed in Saudi Arabia in preparation for a war with Iraq. Most Saudi citizens were aware of the Al Saud family's close relationship with the United States, but few of them were prepared for the arrival of such a large foreign force. To many opponents of the Al Saud family, the decision to station American forces on Saudi soil indicated the degree to which the monarchy had mismanaged its defenses and its economy.

The American-led forces repelled the Iraqi army from Kuwait by the end of March 1991, ending an immediate threat to the government of King Fahd and restoring peace to the region. However, the presence of foreign troops in Saudi Arabia incited the ire of many opposition groups there, who considered the American bases—which remain in Saudi Arabia as of this writing—a desecration of Islamic holy lands. Several of the opposition groups that emerged during the 1990s to challenge the authority of the Saudi monarchy were moderate, but the strongest challenge came from a group of former Afghan mujahideen led by Osama bin Laden, a member of one of Saudi Arabia's wealthiest families.

Al-Qaeda: The World's Most Notorious Terrorist Organization

Bin Laden and several other veterans of the Afghan war against the Soviets were deeply distressed when King Fahd called on the United States to protect his kingdom instead of turning to the battle-tested mujahideen. The veterans from Afghanistan felt they were sufficiently battle tested to repel any invasion from Saddam Hussein, obviating the need for outside intervention. More importantly, they felt an indigenous army of mujahideen was well suited to protect the sanctity of Islam from the encroachment of outside influences, including hostile political regimes in the Arab world. Bin Laden reacted to Fahd's decision to seek U.S. aid by forming his own "army," a conservative Islamic group called al-Qaeda (the Base).

Ironically, al-Qaeda is committed to the same Wahhabi religious principles that were instrumental in Ibn Saud's successful conquest of the Arabian Peninsula during the first half of the twentieth century. However, bin Laden and his adherents felt the Saudi monarchy was no longer sufficiently committed to the religious doctrines that had provided it with a justification for controlling the Arabian Peninsula since its inception. Not only did he believe they were no longer committed to these principles, but bin Laden also felt that the royal family's policies, both foreign and domestic, corrupted the purity of Muslims in Saudi Arabia. As a result, bin Laden and his organization devoted themselves to the expulsion of American troops from Saudi Arabia and the overthrow of the Saudi government.

In order to achieve these goals, al-Qaeda authored some of the most notorious acts of international terrorism during the last decade of the twentieth century. In 1993 al-Qaeda set off bombs in the basement of New York's World Trade Center, and in 1996 it attacked American military bases at the Al Khobar Towers in Riyadh. After a poorly planned American military strike against an al-Qaeda cell in the Sudan, bin Laden and some of his closest advisers issued their infamous fatwa (religious decree) in 1998, declaring war on American citizens and military personnel all over the world. Bin Laden delivered his promise of war on Americans, attacking the American warship USS *Cole* off the coast of Yemen during the fall of 2000 and masterminding the terrorist attacks on New York and Washington, D.C., that forever changed international politics in September 2001.

The development of this organization is linked to a number of historical events, and as a result it is difficult to make generalizations about the root causes of its rise to international prominence. However, it is clear that conditions inside Saudi Arabia had a significant impact on the growth of al-Qaeda and the appeal of its message. Since its creation, the Saudi government has asserted its heritage as protector of the holy cities of Mecca and Medina, and it has also actively encouraged the spread of a conservative strand of Islamic thought that stresses a strict adherence to the Koran and *shariah*. At several points in history, Ibn Saud and his descendants were compelled to support the principles of Wahhabism and encourage its expansion in order to extend their control and influence on the Arabian Peninsula. The Saudi monarchy is, in some ways, responsible for establishing the ideological foundation from which its most committed opponents operate.

Not only did the Saudi government contribute to the ideological agenda of its opponents, but it also provided them with reasons to challenge its commitment to Islamic principles. Several times in the past, Saudi rulers looked to the West for new technologies and technical assistance to advance their pragmatic political goals, which included military protection and expanding the oil industry. As Western technologies, ideas, and armies encroached on Saudi society, the delicate balance between tradition and change in Saudi Arabia began to unravel. At the beginning of the twenty-first century, the unraveling of this balance threatens the legitimacy of the Saudi monarchy and the safety and security of citizens in every region of the world.

The Major Challenges for Contemporary Saudi Arabia

The remainder of this book considers a variety of issues that are linked to the conflict between Saudi traditions and change induced by contact with Western technologies and belief systems. One of these issues is how far Saudi Arabia's leaders should go in order to restrain Islamic fundamentalism, not only within their own borders but also throughout the rest of the Middle East. Deciding to cooperate with the United States and its allies in the war on terror could jeopardize the Al Saud family's Islamic credentials and threaten its legitimacy at home. Failing to cooperate with the United States could also threaten Saudi authority by encouraging intervention from the world's only economic and military superpower. If it is to make a successful transition from the pre–September 11 to the post–September 11 world, Saudi Arabia must find a way to maintain its status as one of the most influential Islamic countries in the world without encouraging the proliferation of fundamentalist groups devoted to the violent overthrow of the existing world order.

Saudi leaders must also address the growing international and domestic demands for domestic political reform. This is especially true with regard to women's rights and religious freedom, which have received greater attention since the September 11 attacks. Many analysts blame Saudi Arabia's conservative religious establishment and its support of radical Islamic groups for the spread of fundamentalist ideologies in the Middle East and South Asia. Internal reform with regard to issues like women's rights and religious freedom might reverse this trend and promote peace and stability in the region. However, reforming the political system and curbing the power of religious elites also carry a heavy price. Drastic reforms would likely mobilize conservative religious groups into a competition for political power with the Al Saud family, potentially destabilizing Saudi Arabia and the rest of the Middle East even more.

Naturally, the situation inside Saudi Arabia is constantly changing and difficult to capture in its entirety, but the goal of this book is to give its readers a snapshot of Saudi Arabia as it stands at the threshold between its turbulent past and its uncertain future. More importantly, it is intended to provide insight into some of the most pressing issues in contemporary international politics that shape the world in which we all live.

CHAPTER 1

The Historical Roots of Saudi Arabia's Current Tensions

Wahhabi Islam and the Rise of the Al Saud Monarchy

By Ayman Al-Yassini

*In the eighteenth century, long before the modern Saudi state was formed in 1932, a movement to reform the religious practices of Muslims on the Arabian Peninsula began. Its leader, Muhammad Ibn Abd al-Wahhab, felt that Muslims in the area had strayed from the teachings of the prophet Muhammad and determined that he must restore the rule of Islamic law (*shariah*) to the peninsula. Ayman Al-Yassini, formerly a staff fellow in political science at the center for developing area studies at McGill University, describes the career of Wahhab and his alliance with Muhammad Ibn Saud, the first Saudi monarch. The alliance fused the military and temporal power of the Al Saud family with the religious authority of Wahhab and his followers. It also laid the foundation for the modern political institutions of Saudi Arabia, which continue to rely on the support of conservative Wahhabi religious leaders for their legitimacy. Many analysts claim that Saudi Arabia's commitment to the teachings of Wahhab contributed to the rise of Islamic fundamentalism and terrorist activity at the end of the twentieth century.*

Eighteenth-century Arabia existed within the domain of the Ottoman empire. Ottoman officials, however, did not exercise effective control beyond the regions bordering the Red Sea and the pilgrimage route to [Mecca and Medina]. Najd and the area eastward led a sovereign form of existence in which the various districts were ruled by local chiefs. The region was characterized by political fragmentation and incessant tribal conflicts. Religious beliefs and practices had deviated from Orthodox Islam. The Najdi historian Ibn Bishr wrote in the eighteenth century that

Ayman Al-Yassini, *Religion and the State in the Kingdom of Saudi Arabia*. Boulder, CO: Westview Press, 1985. Copyright © 1985 by Westview Press, Inc. Reproduced by permission.

it was common for trees and rocks to be invested with supernatural powers; tombs were venerated and shrines were built near them; and all were regarded as sources of blessing and objects of vows. . . . Moreover, swearing by other than God, and similar forms of both major and minor polytheism were widely practiced [among Muslims].

It was into this environment that Muhammad Ibn Abd al-Wahhab was born in 1703, in al-Uyayna in Najd. He belonged to a prestigious family of jurists, both theologians and *qadis* (judges). Under the tutorship of his father, young Muhammad studied Hanbali jurisprudence and read classical works on *tafsir* (exegesis), *hadith* (tradition), and *tawhid* (monotheism). In his early twenties, Muhammad began to denounce what he described as the polytheistic beliefs and practices of his society. He rejected "the corruption and laxity of the contemporary decline . . . [and] insisted solely on the [*shari'ah* (Islamic law)]."

The beliefs of Muhammad Ibn Abd al-Wahhab alienated him from the establishment ulama [religious leaders] and led to the dismissal of his father from the *qada* (judgeship). Subsequently, Ibn Abd al-Wahhab's family, including his father had to leave al-Uyayna for neighboring Huraymila in 1726. Muhammad remained in al-Uyayna for a while, but because the ulama "were able to defame his call and reputation, and instigate the common folk who beset him with ridicule, abuse, and insults," he left al-Uyayna for Hejaz.

In Hejaz, Muhammad made his pilgrimage to Mecca and Medina, where he attended lectures on different branches of Islamic learning. The historian Ibn Bishr reported that he studied under Shaykh Abd Allah Ibn Ibrahim Ibn Sayf and Shaykh Hayat al-Sindi, both of whom were admirers of the Hanbali Ibn Taymiya. Like Ibn Taymiya, Sayf and Sindi opposed *taqlid* (imitation), which was commonly accepted by the followers of the four Sunni schools of jurisprudence. Both scholars felt the urgent need to reform the socioreligious situation of Muslims in Najd and elsewhere. Their teachings had a great impact on Muhammad, who began to take a more aggressive attitude toward the establishment ulama. . . .

Wahhabism Gains Influence

The year 1740 witnessed the death of Muhammad Ibn Abd al-Wahhab's father and the consolidation of the Wahhabi movement. The death of his father allowed the shaykh to adopt a more aggressive line, because he felt less constrained than before. He declared war on those who by word or act were violating the doctrine of monotheism. In a relatively short time, the influence of Muhammad Ibn Abd al-Wahhab spread widely. The consolidation of his movement took place when the ruler of al-Uyayna, Uthman Ibn Mu'ammar, offered him protection. The shaykh accepted the invitation to reside in al-Uyayna both because it allowed him to return to the place of his birth where his family enjoyed a high social status and because it provided the protection he needed to propagate his ideology. To cement his ties with the town's leader, the shaykh married al-Jawhara, Uthman's aunt.

The ruler of al-Uyayna ordered his townsmen to observe the teachings of Muhammad Ibn Abd al-Wahhab. Once the protection of a political leader was secured, the shaykh implemented the principles of his call. Among his earliest acts was the destruction of the spot where Zayd Ibn al-Khatab was believed to be buried, as well as the tombs of other Companions of the Prophet Muhammad, all of whom were objects of veneration. He also revived the Islamic law of stoning an adulterous woman to death. Both incidents mark the establishment of a Wahhabi society in which the doctrines of *tawhid* were strictly observed.

The shaykh's activities, and the protection he received from the leader of al-Uyayna, antagonized the ulama of the region and led them to intensify their attacks on the Wahhabi movement. . . .

The shaykh accused the ulama of opposing his movement because they feared the loss of social prestige and reputation. He reproached them for not taking the initiative in criticizing offensive practices that he considered un-Islamic. He also attributed the opposition of the ulama to his denunciation of the acceptance by the *qadis* of payment from persons who sought their legal advice or arbitration. The ulama of the region intensified their attacks on the shaykh and warned the rulers that "it was their obligation, as Muslim leaders responsible for the preservation of the shari'ah, to put an end to Wahhabi errors and innovations." Pointing to the threatening character of the movement, the ulama noted that the shaykh's purpose was "nothing less than to stir up the common folks to revolt against the authority of the established leaders."

The appeal to eliminate the Wahhabi movement found a positive response from Sulayman Ibn Muhammad, tribal leader of the Bano Khalid and ruler of the al-Ahsa region. Sulayman was concerned with the rapidly increasing number of followers who joined the Wahhabis. Ibn Bishr noted that Sulayman wrote to Uthman Ibn Mu'ammad, ruler of al-Uyayna, demanding that the shaykh be expelled or killed. If not, Sulayman warned, all economic assistance to al-Uyayna would be cut off. Fearful of Sulayman's reprisal, the ruler of al-Uyayna terminated his alliance with the shaykh and expelled him from the town.

The Wahhabi-Saudi Alliance

After his expulsion from al-Uyayna, Ibn Abd al-Wahhab sought refuge in Dar'iya. Its rulers were in conflict with Sulayman Ibn Muhammad, and, more important, the shaykh's doctrine had already been adopted by some notables of the town, among whom were the brothers and sons of Muhammad Ibn Saud, the ruler.

Shortly after his arrival in Dar'iya, the shaykh was visited by Muhammad Ibn Saud, who offered him "protection equal to that of the chief's own women and children." In return for his support, the ruler of Dar'iya asked the shaykh not to leave Dar'iya once other towns began following his teachings and not to oppose his taxation of the inhabitants of the principality. Ibn Abd al-Wahhab agreed to the first condition but, reluctant to give a clear answer to the second he said: ". . . may God grant you victories, the booty from which will be greater than these taxes." The agreement arrived at between the shaykh and the prince may be considered the cornerstone of the Wahhabi-Saudi alliance, according to which, as indicated by the author of *Lam' al-Shihab*, the temporal power was left to Muhammad Ibn Saud and his successors whereas the spiritual was reserved for Muhammad Ibn Abd al-Wahhab and his descendants.

The shaykh spent the first two years at Dar'iya propagating his views and writing letters to various rulers, scholars, and tribal leaders of the peninsula. The response he elicited was as much a product of political and economic considerations as it was a matter of religious dogma. Some leaders joined the new movement because they saw it as a means of gaining an ally against their local rivals. Others feared that their acceptance of the call would diminish their authority in favor of Ibn Saud and oblige them to pay him at least part of the revenues that they collected from their subjects.

By 1746, the time seemed ripe for Al Saud and the shaykh to resort to force in order to achieve what they had not been able to do by means of persuasion and argument. The shaykh's prestige was now firmly established. The inhabitants of the region had been indoctrinated to believe that opponents of the Wahhabi cause were enemies of Islam who should be fought and whose properties were lawful spoil.

Since the region was beyond the reach of organized political authority, it offered the Wahhabis the opportunity to pursue their designs by military means. Muhammad Ibn Abd al-Wahhab and Muhammad Ibn Saud declared *jihad* (holy war) on their opponents. One principality after another fell under the attacks of the Saudi forces. By 1773 the principality of Riyadh had fallen, and its properties were incorporated by the treasury of Dar'iya.

The fall of Riyadh marked a new period in the career of Muhammad Ibn Abd al-Wahhab. He delegated some of his power to Abd al-Aziz Ibn Muhammad Ibn Saud, who succeeded his father in 1765, and concentrated on teaching and worship until his death in 1791. The death of Muhammad Ibn Abd al-Wahhab did not stop the expansion of the new state, however. The movement not only resisted its opponents and gained territories in neighboring principalities, but it was also able, within a relatively short period, to subjugate both Mecca and Medina, which were captured in 1805 and 1806, respectively. . . .

The Durability of the Saudi-Wahhabi Alliance

When Muhammad Ibn Abd al-Wahhab began his movement in the 1720s, his immediate objectives were to gain recognition and protection from a political leader in the Arabian Peninsula. The alliance he forged with Prince Muhammad Al Saud in 1740 fulfilled both objectives. It provided Al Saud with an ideological rationalization of their rule in Arabia.

Once the Saudi state became institutionalized, the shaykh continued to play an important role in the affairs of the polity. Indeed, Al Saud found the doctrinal formulations of Ibn Abd al-Wahhab to be highly instrumental in the propagation of their rule. The dependency on religious movements for legitimacy of Muslim political leaders, including the Saudis of the eighteenth century, is not surprising. The Abbasid and Fatimid caliphs [Islamic rulers], for example, came to power on the crest of religious movements. What is surprising, however, is that the relationship between religion and state in eighteenth-century Arabia was harmonious. Both the religious and political spheres shared a complementarity of objectives. The existence of one was dependent on the survival and continued support of the other. The durability of this alliance, however, needs to be tested by reference to twentieth-century developments, when Ibn Saud resurrected the Saudi kingdom in 1932. The question is this: To what extent can the modern state, given its monopoly of force and resources and its need to maintain a high level of autonomy, tolerate an autonomous religious domain that could compete with it for loyalty?

The Birth of Saudi Arabia

By Madawi Al-Rasheed

The Al Saud family, a formidable power on the Arabian Peninsula since the fifteenth century, briefly expanded beyond their traditional area of influence in the village of Diriyya in the late eighteenth and early nineteenth centuries. However, it was not until 1903 that the process to consolidate the Arabian Peninsula under the control of the Al Saud began in earnest. Madawi Al-Rasheed, a senior lecturer in social anthropology at King's College in London, recounts the process of unification under the direction of Saudi Arabia's founder, Ibn Saud. Al-Rasheed argues that the successful ascent of the Saudi family was the result of a combination of several factors that included the leadership of Ibn Saud as well as the efforts of the British to influence developments on the peninsula after the First World War. The combination of internal dynamics and external influences eventually led to the establishment of the Kingdom of Saudi Arabia in 1932.

The dominant narrative in the history of Saudi Arabia in the twentieth century is that of state formation, a process that started in the interior of Arabia under the leadership of the Al Sa'ud. While this leadership was not new (it was visible in the history of Arabia in the eighteenth and nineteenth centuries), the modern state of 1932 distinguished itself by creating a stable and durable realm that successfully incorporated Hijaz, 'Asir and Hasa, in addition to the central province of Najd. The state brought diverse people and vast territories under its authority as a result of a long campaign of conquest.

In its early days the course taken by the new state resembles a cycle familiar in the region. Since the eighteenth century, several ambitious local rulers (from the Al Sa'ud and others) had tried to expand their authority over adjacent territories, but their attempts failed for

Madawi Al-Rasheed, *A History of Saudi Arabia*. Cambridge, UK: Cambridge University Press, 2002. Copyright © 2002 by Cambridge University Press. Reproduced by permission.

a variety of reasons. The Al Sa°ud and other local rulers founded polities which were, however, destroyed shortly after they reached a substantial level of expansion. Given this historical background, the state of 1932 is often seen as a success story. In this story the legendary figure of °Abd al°Aziz ibn °Abd al-Rahman Al Sa°ud (thereafter Ibn Sa°ud), the founder of the Kingdom of Saudi Arabia, is dominant. The fact that his state has not vanished as so many earlier emirates did adds to the credibility of the story. . . .

The Arabian Peninsula Under Ottoman Rule

In the nineteenth century, there were several attempts to bring more of Arabia under direct Ottoman rule. The Ottoman-Egyptian invasion of Arabia in 1818 and the Ottoman occupation of Hasa and °Asir in 1871 were meant to establish direct Ottoman authority in the peninsula. However, vast territories remained without an Ottoman governor. Several local amirs in the interior were recognised as 'ruling on behalf of the Sultan' and occasionally they were sent subsidies and gifts to cement alliance and ensure obedience. The Ottomans expected local rulers to restrain their followers from attacking pilgrimage caravans and Ottoman garrisons stationed in more vital regions, for example in Hijaz and Hasa.

This situation was maintained until the defeat of the Ottoman Empire during the First World War. While Sharif Husayn of Hijaz actively supported Britain against the Ottomans, other influential rulers distanced themselves from a war that did not closely influence their domains. Ibn Rashid in Ha'il declared his allegiance to the Ottoman Sultan without offering any serious military support, while Ibn Sa°ud in Riyadh sided with the British without being directly involved in the war against the Ottomans.

What was to become of Arabia after the collapse of the Ottoman Empire after the First World War? When France and Britain partitioned Ottoman territories under the mandate system, Arabia fell within Britain's sphere of influence. Arabia, however, was not to become a colony similar to other colonies in the British Empire. During the war, Britain cultivated intimate relationships with two main local powers, Sharif Husayn and Ibn Sa°ud, but failed to reconcile their claims to rule Arabia after the war. Britain's conflicting policies and promises together with its financial support strengthened both rulers. The idea that Arabia could be unified became more realistic, now that there were only two strong rivals, one in Hijaz and one in Najd. The throne of Sharif Husayn was sacrificed in favour of Ibn

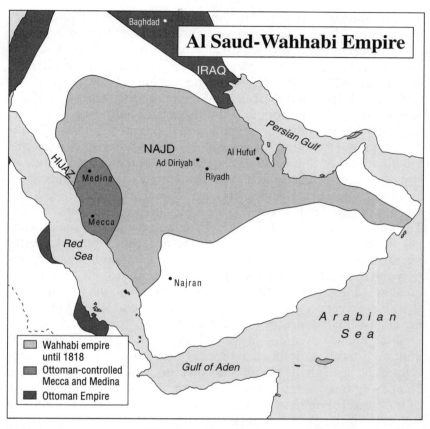

Sa°ud, who took over Hijaz in 1925, ousting the Sharifian family in the process. In 1932, Ibn Sa°ud declared himself king and his realm the Kingdom of Saudi Arabia.

Britain's Role in the Ascendance of Ibn Saud

Najd's nominal incorporation in the Ottoman Empire and the fact that it did not become a colony similar to other Arab countries in the twentieth century led many scholars to comment on its unique history. Its modern state is often considered as an indigenous formation assisted by the unique efforts of its founder, Ibn Sa°ud. While Saudi Arabia did not inherit a colonial administration or a nationalist elite similar to that developed elsewhere in the Arab world, one must not exaggerate its so-called unique history. Britain did not turn Saudi Arabia into a colony, but British influence during the first three decades of the twentieth century was paramount. It is difficult to imagine Ibn Sa'ud successfully conquering one region after another without British subsidies. The weakened Ottoman Empire accepted his conquest of Hasa in 1913. Unable to reverse the situation, the Ottomans recognised Ibn Sa'ud as the *de facto* ruler of Najd. Britain later sanctioned this in 1915 when she recognised that 'Najd, Hasa, Qatif, and Jubayl and their dependencies are the territories of Ibn Sa'ud'. Similarly, his conquest of the Rashidi emirate in 1921 was only possible with British weapons and generous subsidies. His expansion into Hijaz in 1925 took place at a time when Britain was growing tired of Sharif Husayn's demands, perceived as a threat to British interests. Britain was more than happy to see Sharif Husayn removed from Hijaz, leaving his sons, Faysal and 'Abdullah, on the thrones of two newly created monarchies in Trans-Jordan and Iraq. Throughout the 1920s and 1930s, Britain remained the main external player behind the formation of the Sa'udi state. While Saudi Arabia escaped some of the ruptures of direct colonial rule, state formation and the unification of Arabia under Sa'udi leadership must be understood in the context of British intervention in the Middle East. Britain's influence weakened only after the Second World War, when the USA began to assume a greater role.

To argue, however, that the Sa'udi state of 1932 was a British 'invention' misses an important aspect of the internal dynamics that shaped the state and led to its consolidation. While Britain may have been a key force behind state formation, the rise and consolidation of the Sa'udi state resulted from a complex process that cannot be traced to any single external factor.

The Process of Unifying Saudi Arabia

The twentieth century witnessed the emergence of a state imposed on people without a historical memory of unity or national heritage which would justify their inclusion in a single entity. With the exception of a substantial Shi'a minority in Hasa, the majority of Sa'udis are Sunni Muslims. The population, however, had been divided by regional and tribal differences that militated against national unity or unification. Saudi Arabia shared this important characteristic with several Arab countries that came into being during the period between the two great wars. While the borders of many Arab states were drawn in accordance with French and British policies, the four regions that comprised Saudi Arabia (Najd, Hasa, Hijaz and 'Asir) were 'unified' as a result of their conquest by an indigenous leadership, sanctioned by a colonial power.

The unification of Arabia under the leadership of Ibn Sa'ud was a process that lasted some thirty years. Between 1902 and 1932, Ibn

Saʿud defeated several rivals until his realm reached the limits acceptable to Britain. Where France had been the colonial power, republics emerged. But in Saudi Arabia a kingdom was founded, as in parts of the Arab world where Britain had been influential, namely Trans-Jordan and Iraq.

Saudi Arabia is, however, different from other Arab countries. The conquests of Ibn Saʿud did not proceed under nationalistic rhetoric or the discourse of independence and self-rule. With the exception of Hijaz, where such rhetoric emerged during the Arab revolt (1916) associated with Sharif Husayn who aspired to become 'King of the Arabs', the rest of Saudi Arabia had no experience of such aspirations. Moreover, Britain did not distinguish herself by great efforts to generate discourses on independence and autonomy.

The conquest of Arabia by an indigenous ruler took place with a very different symbolic vocabulary. Ibn Saʿud relied on ancestral claims to rule over a region that 'once belonged to his ancestors'. When he returned to Riyadh from his exile in Kuwait in 1902, he was merely restoring or extending the Al Saʿud claim over the town. Similarly, further expansion in Qasim, Hasa, northern Najd, Hijaz and ʿAsir was undertaken with the intention of restoring his family's authority over territories that had been once incorporated under Saʿudi leadership. This was a reference to the short-lived experience of the eighteenth century when the first Saʿudi-Wahhabi emirate (1744–1818) succeeded briefly in stretching the limits of Saʿudi rule beyond their small provincial capital, Dirʿiyyah. This historical precedent proved to be a justification for expansion in the early decades of the twentieth century.

Alone, however, this justification fell short of convincing Ibn Saʿud's local rivals to accept his rule. Force was mightier than vague ancestral claims. Most regions were incorporated in Ibn Saʿud's realm only after he had overcome the resistance of local leadership. Coercion proceeded in tandem with the revival of Wahhabism, the reformist movement that once inspired the people of southern Najd to expand beyond the interior of Arabia. As early as 1902, Ibn Saʿud enlisted the *mutawwaʿa* (religious ritual specialists) of Najd, in the process of expansion. The *mutawwaʿa* were behind the formation of the *ikhwan*, a tribal military force that was dedicated to fight in the name of *jihad* (holy war) against the 'infidels', a loosely defined category that at times included people who were not easily persuaded to accept Saʿudi leadership.

The project of unifying Arabia was a gradual process assisted by several factors that were beyond the control of Ibn Saʿud. The defeat of the Ottoman Empire in the First World War and the encouragement of Britain allowed Ibn Saʿud to fill a power vacuum in Arabia. The unification of vast territories under his rule after he had secured Riyadh in 1902 could not easily have been anticipated. The popular historiography of this period tends to paint a picture of Ibn Saʿud as a 'desert warrior' who had the genius and foresight from the very beginning. It took thirty years of warfare and more than fifty-two battles between 1902 and 1932 before the project materialised. The idea of a Saʿudi state was a late development, certainly not associated with Ibn Saʿud's early conquests. . . .

Islamic Traditions and Modernization in Saudi Arabia

Crucial to any understanding of modern Saʿudi history is the observation that this history shows a striking accommodation between the old and the new. Saudi Arabia's position as the location of the holiest shrines of Islam is at the heart of this accommodation. This has meant that Saʿudi internal politics and society are not only the concern of its own rather small population, but also the concern of millions of Muslims in the world. The symbolic significance of Saudi Arabia for Islam and Muslims cannot be overestimated. It has become a prerogative for its people and state to preserve its Islamic heritage. It is also a prerogative to cherish the responsibilities of geographical accident which has made it the destination not only of Muslim pilgrims but also the direction for their five daily prayers. The country's transformation in the twentieth century is shaped by this important fact that required a careful and reluctant immersion in modernity. The preservation of the 'old', the 'authentic' tradition progressed with an eye on the 'new', the 'modern' and the 'alien'. Saudi Arabia's specific Islamic tradition, namely Wahhabi teachings, did not encourage an easy immersion in modernity in the twentieth century. From the very beginning, the ruling group stumbled across several obstacles when they introduced the most simple of technologies (for example, cars, the telegraph and television among other innovations). Objections from conservative religious circles were overcome as a result of a combination of force and negotiations. Social and political change proved more problematic and could not be easily implemented without generating debates that threatened the internal stability of the country and alienated important and influential sections of society.

In addition to its specific religious heritage, modern Saudi Arabia emerged against the social, economic and political diversity of its population. The cosmopolitan Hijaz and Hasa with their long history of contact with the outside world were incorporated into the interior, a region that assumed hegemony with the consolidation of the modern state in spite of its relative isolation throughout the previous two hundred years. The social values and political tradition of Najd were generalised to the whole country after 1932. Resistance to rapid social and political change had always been generated in Najd, where the most conservative elements in society continue to be found even at the beginning of the twenty-first century. A combination of a strong tribal tradition in the interior, together with a strict interpretation of Islam in the major towns and oases, made this region most resistant to *bid⁻a*, 'innovations or heresy'. Given that the Al Sa⁻ud's leadership had always been based on the allegiance of the sedentary communities of Najd, the *hadar*, their rule was dependent on accommodating this region's interests, aspirations and political tradition.

The accommodation between the old and the new became more urgent with the discovery of huge quantities of oil under Saudi Arabia's desert territories. With oil, the Sa⁻udi state began to have unprecedented wealth at its disposal to build its economic and material infrastructure and transform its landscape beyond recognition. In the process, both state and society faced an urgent challenge. Can the 'old' Najdi tradition be preserved? Can it coexist with a juxtaposition of the 'new'? These questions proved to be especially difficult in a society that has undergone rapid modernisation. How to benefit from oil wealth while remaining faithful to Islam and tradition has generated unresolved tensions that have accompanied state and nation building since the early 1930s. Colonialism or its absence is irrelevant because Saudi Arabia has been drawn into the international context and world power politics since the early decades of the twentieth century. With the discovery of oil in the 1930s, Saudi Arabia's incorporation in the world economy became an important aspect of its historical development.

The Discovery of Oil and Social Change in Saudi Arabia

By Anders Jerichow

Anders Jerichow, the foreign editor for the Dutch newspaper Politiken, *has spent time in Saudi Arabia interviewing dissidents and political prisoners in an effort to uncover the human rights situation in the desert kingdom. Jerichow describes the tensions and changes visited on Saudi society and Saudi political institutions after the discovery of oil in 1937. Prior to becoming a major oil producer, Saudi Arabia was of little importance to the major world powers of the time and was able to retain its traditional, nomadic social order. After the discovery of oil, Saudi Arabia was transformed as the majority of Saudis resettled in large cities and foreign corporations set up joint ventures with the Saudi monarchy designed to extract and distribute Saudi oil to Western markets. Initially, these changes produced enormous benefits for the Saudi population, such as improved health care and social services. However, the increased contact with other cultures and the instability of world oil prices have combined to produce tension between the conservative religious elite and younger Saudis who want to see significant changes in Saudi Arabia's political and economic systems.*

To an urban dweller the desert seems silent and inviolable. Sand gets in your eyes when the wind blows; it absorbs moisture at night, and water when it rains, only to return to its dry, inviolable state when the sun comes out again. But as any Bedouin knows the

Anders Jerichow, *Saudi Arabia: Outside Global Law and Order, a Discussion Paper*. Richmond, UK: Curzon Press, 1997. Copyright © 1997 by Anders Jerichow. Reproduced by permission of the publisher.

desert is alive and its contours are constantly changing, although it always retains its true identity.

So, too, is Saudi Arabia: a classical Bedouin society in the Arabian desert until the middle of this century, since then the home of hefty economic development which has turned Bedouins into urban dwellers, nomadic herdsmen to modern super-farmers and desert warriors into uniformed soldiers. Nevertheless, they still retain their true identity. This was Saudi Arabia's message when the Ministry of Information in Riyadh inserted advertisements in the international media on 23 September 1992, celebrating '60 years of progress without change'.

Ironically, Saudi Arabia was one of the few countries in the Middle East never to be colonised or to have its borders defined by the imperial powers, because then it was not considered strategically important. Britain and France and the Ottoman Empire had been extremely busy feathering their nests in countries like Egypt, Syria, Lebanon, Palestine, Jordan, Iraq and the tribal nations along the Arabian Gulf. On the other side of 'Rub al-Khiali', or the 'empty corner' of the desert, Aden—in what was later to become South Yemen—had long been of strategic importance because of its good harbour on the imperial route to Southern and Eastern Asia. But the heart of the peninsula was not given much attention by the colonial powers, precisely because of the desert and its remoteness from everything that otherwise tempted hungry empires.

The idea of the world's great powers landing half a million soldiers on the peninsula in 1991/92 to defend this desert and secure the freedom of the little neighbouring emirate of Kuwait would have sounded like a very tall story in the first half of [the twentieth] century.

While the imperial powers competed for the rest of the Middle East, the only ones to be fighting on the Arabian Peninsula were the tribal chiefs. They fought for power over and control of the fulcrum of the Arab tradition in the birthplace of the Prophet in Mecca and the town of Medina, where he founded his Islamic empire and where he was later buried.

One of the tribe or clan leaders, Abdel-Aziz Ibn Saud, who was allied to some of the most orthodox devotees of the puritan Wahhabi sect, had the fortune and the necessary military ingenuity in 1932 to found the enormous kingdom which he named after his own family.

The Discovery of Oil

Saudi Arabia was born and its significance became clear to the international powers in 1937 when the first oil wells showed that the desert concealed incredible wealth in the form of 'black gold'. The vast majority of Saudi Arabia's population were nomadic Bedouins, engaged in trade across the desert and the peninsula or looking after their flocks and small farms, of which only those in mountain regions received enough rain to have any permanence.

The oil was to make such a difference—although only a material one initially—that Saudi Arabia's ruling family and the clergy, who were accustomed to living in isolation from the rest of the world (including the Muslim world) were not interested in opening the country's borders to outside cultural influence.

If that was their ambition, it also became a huge dilemma for Saudi Arabia, especially after oil income started seriously to tempt material change. The clergy found no sympathy for cars, telephones, television or the computers of the modern age. All of it was conceived as inroads by a faithless world outside into the Islamism of the Saud family. But—allegiance with the Wahhabi sect or no—the ruling Saud family was in no mind to miss out on the possibilities the new world had to offer, neither in the form of weaponry to defend borders the Saud family had set, nor in the form of the social development, which the family was now able to buy with its oil money. The result was a compromise, which turned out to be the dilemma of the Saud-Wahhabi alliance and the source of its ultimate demise.

Oil revenues, social development and new technology were quickly followed by new forms of education and, unavoidably, by new conceptions of the age and its prospects. From the point of view of the secular royal power it was a question of welfare. From the clergy's point of view, though, it represented a threat to the authoritarian interpretation of Islam and a temptation to be seduced by subversion from the outside world. Their compromise involved the acceptance by the clergy of the entire new social, educational and technological revolution, which was to be implemented 'without change' to the power structure. Saudi Arabia would, like the desert, maintain its identity and its inviolability under the uncircumventable banner of Wahhabi Islam.

Dramatic Changes in Saudi Society

The material and social development, which was moderate to begin with, became almost explosive in the 1970s. The old Bedouin community which accounted for the majority of the population two decades earlier, had been reduced to just 10 per cent by the late 1970s.

The influx to the towns was enormous—two-thirds of the population were suddenly urban—with all that entails in terms of the demand for new housing, new industries and jobs, schools and health services. Only the explosion in the international price of oil in the wake of the Israeli-Arab October war in 1973 enabled Saudi Arabia's rulers to avoid serious dislocation.

It was not that there was a lack of things to be done. Roads, housing, schools and hospitals were built, and public administrations and private companies were established. But Saudi Arabia's own citizens were only prepared to enjoy the fruits of development, not work towards it, as they were not yet trained to do the jobs that needed to be done. Instead, millions of foreign workers and experts were imported; unskilled workers from Southern Asia and the Far East, middle-ranking technicians from other Arab countries in the Middle East and fully-trained so-called 'experts' from the West.

Instead of waiting for Saudi workers to complete their training, the royal family in Riyadh used its new oil billions to guarantee both training and occupations for their own citizens. All children attended school and young people were offered higher education. Young Saudi couples were given economic assistance to set up home. Health care was free and local transport prices kept low with enormous subsidies. Everything money could buy was bought in the 1970s: new roads, new weaponry, new palaces for the royal family, new oil installations—even farms were transplanted into an environment where before they would have been mirages. . . .

Outside Influences

The dilemma of the power-policy compromise [between the monarchy and clergy] was not something that could simply be cast off. Saudi Arabia's new educational system did not exactly live up to international standards of creativity and critical thinking. Instead, it stuck to tradition with the emphasis on learning by role and respect for prevailing authority. All the same, the new learning did create new demands for more information and material change.

Although the country's boundaries were still closed to tourism and to free entry and departure, the Saud family had invited so many guest workers and 'experts' into the country that every third individual in the kingdom was a foreigner. They had no ties with either the traditions of Saudi Arabia or Wahhabi interpretations of Islam. Both from within and without, the seeds had been sown for demands and expectations for other ways of life than that based on established Bedouin tradition.

The Saud dynasty had promised the clerics that they would maintain the nation's moral codes and keep the amorality of the West at bay, but the leaders of the Saud dynasty were well acquainted with other ways of living than in the shadow of the mosque and the renunciation of earthly pleasures. The younger generation of the dynasty were sent in large numbers to the USA and Britain to get the best education.

The Oil Boom of the 1970s

During the first decade after the oil boom in 1973–74, developments led to some coarse-grained contrasts: huge numbers of effectively unemployed, state-subsidised Saudi Arabians living side by side with underpaid guest workers, increasing numbers of fully-trained Saudi Arabians without the prospect of employment in a free labour market, and ever-improving levels of social welfare without its consumers either paying for it or fixing its price.

Most of the oil from the world's largest reserves was sent directly to refineries abroad, rather than Saudi Arabia making use of the potential of full employment in oil production. In the meantime, inflation skyrocketed. The public administration employed hoards of Saudi Arabians without demanding anything of them or expecting them to show anything for the salary they were paid.

Deep inside Saudi Arabia this was interpreted by some as an attempt to 'corrupt' the society. Saudi Arabia certainly avoided the slums, unemployment and social frustrations that followed in the wake of rapid urbanisation in countries such as Turkey and numerous Latin-American societies in the 1960s, 1970s and 1980s.

Abroad, Saudi Arabia did not seem to have changed. The men still proudly wore their ankle-length coats and the women their top-to-toe black gowns with only a net in front of the face. But behind the facade and the proud traditions, the same Saudi Arabians had been confronted with international competition in their new education system and a new bombardment of information from the world outside. Moreover, the Saudis had to decide exactly what it was they wanted of their welfare society, which a hereditary royal power had financed, built and corrupted.

This decision might have been delayed by a few more years had the oil pumps only been allowed to work undisturbed. The Saud family had admittedly done what it could to distribute its work-free sources of growing wealth. In other countries, the same system would have been considered corrupt. In Saudi Arabia, however, it became an efficient industry for local Saudis to take a 'commission' for acting as a middleman (it required no work on their part) between foreign companies and Saudi Arabia. As early as 1977 it was decided that no Saudi should, officially, represent more than 10 foreign companies. This distributed work-free incomes which, until then, had made members of the royal family immensely rich.

Although they were legal in Saudi Arabia, these incomes still tended to be centred largely on the 5,000 princes and other families with 'access' to those who really hold the power. Equally the 'commission' system gave rise to both religious and secular criticism of growing corruption in the kingdom.

Meanwhile, Saudi Arabia was burdened by two Gulf wars. In the first of these—between Iraq and non-Arab Iran from 1980–88—the Saud family, out of self-interest, helped the Iraqis with both gifts and loans that were never repaid.

The other Gulf war—following Iraq's invasion of Kuwait in 1990–91—cost Saudi Arabia almost half its financial reserves. It paid the lion's share of having half a million soldiers in the kingdom and the campaign to liberate Kuwait in January and February 1991.

The Saudi Arabia economy was in dire straits and to make matters worse, the war had not forced oil prices up. Saudi Arabia's national income had experienced a drastic fall and the Riyadh government was faced with an unpleasant, unaccustomed budget deficit.

Despite heavy investment in local industry and attempts to spread the nation's income base, oil was in the mid-1990s still the source of three-quarters of the Saudi Arabian government's income. Oil also accounted for more than three-quarters of exports from the kingdom. Drastic measures were decreed by the king in the next five-year plan: the deficit had to go. More Saudi Arabians would have to work, that is, do proper, productive work, with the desired consequence that foreign workers would be sent home and state subsidies to water and electricity and domestic food production would be cut back.

This move was no different than any other government would have made in a similar situation, but Saudi Arabia is not any country. Its population has to a great extent not been accustomed to working for its income, not used to paying cost price for food, water and electricity. Until now, the country's gifts had been seen as rewards for the power the dynasty had reserved for itself. The demand that Saudi Arabians should take over more productive work might act like a boomerang against the ruling dynasty. In other countries it has always been natural for the imposition of taxes to be followed up by demands from those who pay them. Of course, in Saudi Arabia the rulers have been financed more by oil income than taxation, but the oil, too, is public common property. It is written in the law that the oil belongs to the nation and not the Saud dynasty. And if the dynasty starts making demands on its subjects, they may very well start making demands the other way. This will make it extremely difficult for the powers that be to insist on progress without change.

Difficult Changes in Saudi Arabia After the Gulf War

By Sulayman Nyang and Evan Hendricks

In August of 1990, Iraq invaded its southern neighbor Kuwait. Fearing that Iraqi leader Saddam Hussein would also invade his country, King Faud of Saudi Arabia invited the United States to station troops on Saudi soil in order to protect the kingdom from Hussein's advancing columns. In January 1991 the American army used its bases in Saudi Arabia to prosecute what became known as the Gulf War, which ended with the restoration of the Kuwaiti monarchy later that year. In the following excerpt, Sulayman Nyang, professor of African studies at Howard University, and Evan Hendricks, the editor and publisher of Privacy Times, *discuss some of the changes Saudi Arabia experienced as a result of the Gulf War between Iraq and the United States. The war not only created a rift between conservative Muslim groups and liberal political leaders on the issue of stationing American troops in Saudi Arabia, but it also forced the Saudi monarchy to take a more active role in international affairs—something it typically avoided before the war began.*

Throughout history, wars have proven to be a catalyst for change for victorious nations, both domestically and internationally. In some cases, wars have led to revolutionary transformations on both fronts.

For Saudi Arabia, on the one hand, the Gulf War [of 1991] most definitely brought important positive changes to the domestic situation, and to its standing in the international community. On the other hand, many argue that the war did not cause an abrupt alteration in

Saudi Arabia's historical course, but rather only accelerated changes that were destined to occur.

At home, the traditional conflict between the Islamic militants and the more liberal business and professional classes has become more pronounced [since the war]. Fearing that the pro-western tilt would translate into a loosening of the strictly applied Islamic mores from which they derive their authority, the Islamic militants became more aggressive in attacking government policies. Using religious societies, mosques, and bootleg cassette recordings, the militants attacked government decisions to allow stationing of American troops, to support U.S.-sponsored Middle East peace negotiations with Israel and to borrow $10 billion on the international markets.

During the Gulf War, a group of Saudi women staged a protest by engaging in the taboo act of driving their own cars in a suburb of Riyadh. The incident outraged religious conservatives, but was handled deftly by King Fahd.

Both the religious militants and the liberals have been described as vocal fringe groups, relatively small in number, while the majority of Saudis are considered conservative and said to lean more in favor of religious restriction than liberalization.

But the liberals, many of whom are from the business community, insist that the government will have to loosen religious-inspired restrictions on business and social practices if it hopes to create an expanding economic environment capable of meeting the high expectations for opportunity of the emerging generation of young Saudis.

Liberals also complain that militant student groups increasingly are verbally harassing professors and other students that do not share their views. Both sides reportedly are taking advantage of the main Saudi tradition of redress and flooding King Fahd with opposing petitions.

Reforms in the Saudi Legal System

By the end of 1991, the authorities had turned their attention to the militants, who in their underground cassettes had attacked the Saudi Women's Renaissance Association as "prostitutes" and demanded that it be disbanded. Many of the association's members are also members of the Royal Family. The attack provoked a stern response by Prince Turki al-Faisal, who in a speech at a mosque reportedly warned the Iman that he had gone too far, and that they either must prove their charges or be held accountable for making them. The following week, the Iman admitted his guilt and was fired by his superiors.

This event prompted Sheikh Abd al-Aziz Ibn Baz, the highest ranking religious leader, to announce, "Many of those who pretend to have knowledge and a religious calling," he said, "have in this day and age, surfaced to contest and injure established religious leaders, doing so secretly in their gatherings or proclaiming their views openly in sermons in the mosques, or records these views on cassettes that are distributed among the people. I counsel those who have misguided youths and filled them with hatred and conspiracies and erroneous gossip about such and such person, to repent and desist from those activities."

In mid-1992, King Fahd issued a long-awaited order for creation of the national consultative council, and for a bill of rights protecting basic individual freedoms such as privacy, and for the first time revising the way the King is chosen. The reforms, which were the product of a pledge the King made in 1978, were designed to expand participation in government decisionmaking. The council, to which the King appointed sixty members, may slightly favor the business community, as well as the middle class that composes the majority of Saudi society.

Although the reforms did not meet the high standards demanded by some international human rights groups, they were applauded by many foreign governments as important steps toward participatory government and recognition of citizens' rights.

Thus, there was nothing new in the tensions between contrasting wings of the Saudi political spectrum. But the Gulf War certainly intensified competition between them, and accelerated their expression of disagreement. What is new, and yet to be tested, is the legal and administrative framework that the government created to accommodate their formal participation in its decisionmaking.

Expanding Military Cooperation with the United States

Prior to the Gulf War, Saudi Arabia played a modest role in regional politics, often deferring to its more populous neighbors to take center stage. But the war drastically changed the alignment, knocking out Iraq as a regional superpower and creating a vacuum which Saudi Arabia was obliged to fill.

Although Saudi Arabia and the United States were seen as being the closest of allies, Saudi Arabia did not favor "prepositioning" American troops on the Kingdom's soil. The United States military wanted to "preposition" arms and equipment for 150,000 soldiers on Saudi soil, a policy dream that stemmed from the days when pro-Israel hawks like Richard Perle and Stephen Bryen were prominent in the Pentagon.

The United States' push for a "forward headquarters element" in the Kingdom was particularly insensitive, considering that the two sides agreed explicitly at the outset that U.S. troops would leave when the job was finished, and that there was widespread domestic and regional opposition to a continued foreign military presence. What the Saudis naturally wanted was to build up its ground forces so it would no longer be dependent on foreigners for its defense. The Defense Department and the State Department tried to use this as leverage to persuade the Saudis to agree to a new defense cooperative agreement, much like the one Kuwait signed with the U.S. In particular, the State Department indicated that it did not want to sell arms that the Saudi buildup entailed at a time when it was supposed to reduce arms sales in the Middle East.

The Saudis were probably not encouraged by the fact that two of the American officials pushing the prepositioning plan were Defense Undersecretary Paul D. Wolfowitz and Assistant Secretary Richard Clarke, both known for being pro-Israeli. Saudi Ambassador Prince Bandar Ibn Sultan repeatedly rebuffed requests for meetings from Clarke, who subsequently was implicated in a State Department Inspector General report on unauthorized transfers of U.S. technology to Israel. The State Department even moved to reprimand Clarke.

In an ambiguous compromise, the United States and Saudi Arabia in May 1992 settled on an obscure fifteen-year-old military training pact as the legal framework for a broad expansion of strategic cooperation between the two nations, according to the American and Saudi officials interviewed by the *Washington Post.* Known as the 1977 Military Training Mission Treaty, the accord was invoked to justify the stationing of a small number of military advisers in the Gulf region, including Saudi Arabia, as well as storage of support equipment for five or six fighter wings (400 planes) and some tanks and fighting vehicles. The scale of the storage operation is only a fraction of the original prepositioning plan proposed by the Pentagon. Moreover, many details were left for negotiations which promised to drag on well beyond the November 1992 U.S. presidential election, as the Saudis wanted to await the results of those elections before proceeding. The Saudis reportedly made it clear that in no way should the agreement suggest acceptance of a permanent U.S. military base.

On the issue of Iraq, the Saudis were aggressively pressing the United States to carry out a covert action campaign to topple Saddam Hussein. The initiative, according to the *New York Times,* sought an allied effort to supply arms and intelligence to Kurdish rebels in northern Iraq, Shiite Muslim fighters in the south and Sunni Muslim opposition forces in central Iraq. The aim was to draw and divide Saddam Hussein's last Republican Guard divisions protecting his strongholds around Baghdad and subject them to allied air assaults. The plan, which sounded more like a psychological warfare game out of the CIA's "Bay of Pigs Institute for Success Overseas" than a serious operation, apparently was never carried out.

Instead a report surfaced in May 1992 that the CIA was flooding Iraq with counterfeit currency in an attempt to destabilize the government. However, the *New York Times* reported there was no evidence the operation was effecting any real progress towards overthrowing Saddam. The *Times* also reported that the Bush Administration authorized full-fledged covert operations against Iraq in February 1992. While the Saudis undoubtedly benefitted from the close military alliance with the United States during the Gulf War and were impressed by American prowess, they are likely to learn that the successes of CIA covert operations are fewer and farther between.

Saudi-Iranian Competition

While much attention remained on Iraq, the two main competitors for regional influence were Saudi Arabia and Iran [after the Gulf War]. This was an age-old competition, dating back to the origins of the split between Sunni and Shiite Muslims a millennia ago. Iran continues to seek to export its style of Islam, and has the manpower, military equipment, and ten years of [battle] experience in its favor. Iran's main weakness is its anemic economy and risk of growing internal dissension caused by scarcity and dissatisfaction with the ruling Mullahs.

Another factor intensifying the competition between Iran and Saudi Arabia was the breakup of the Soviet Union in 1991 and the quest to be the main Islamic ally of the former Soviet republics of Azerbaijan, Kazakhstan, Kirghizia, Tajikistan, Turkmenistan, and Uzbekistan. Only Azerbaijan was Shiite, while the others were Sunni. Iran has tried emphasizing cultural and religious connections, particularly to Azerbaijan, but has run into stiff competition from Turkey, which in fact has stronger historical and cultural ties with the region, and appeared to be cooperating with Saudi Arabia. . . .

Some observers speculated that the nuclear arena could emerge as another area of competition between the two Islamic regimes. In 1992, former CIA Director Robert M. Gates told Congress that Iran was trying to acquire a nuclear weapons capability, but predicted that this goal was unlikely to be achieved before the year 2000. While Iran officially denied seeking the bomb, some Iranian leaders publicly proclaimed that they would have the first "Islamic" nuclear weapon.

A likely resource for any Mideast nuclear program (aside from Israel's) is the Iraqi nuclear program. The main strength of the Iraqi program was the estimated 4,000 Arabs, many of them Palestinians and Egyptians, who arrived in Baghdad between 1974 and 1977, to work on Saddam's nuclear effort. These engineers and scientists were responding not only to promises of higher pay, but also to the appeal of working in an all-Arab program. One of the leading Iraqi nuclear scientists, Hussein Sharistani, a Shiite, claimed he refused to work on the program when he discovered it was designed to build a bomb. He was arrested in 1979 and tortured and charged with membership in an anti-regime organization. He was sentenced to twenty years in prison but escaped to Iran in 1991 after an allied air raid on Abu Ghraib prison in Baghdad.

The end of the Gulf War led to revelations that shocked the world into realizing how close the Iraqis were to developing the bomb. Is it far-fetched then to speculate that these revelations sparked an intense competition between Iran and Saudi Arabia for the services of these knowledgeable nuclear scientists?

It is worth remembering that the end of World War II set off a similar scramble for Nazi nuclear scientists by two new competitors—the United States and the Soviet Union—and ushered in the nuclear age.

Saudi Arabia Becomes a Regional Power

The Gulf War removed any doubts about Saudi Arabia's ability to convert its oil-based economic wealth into political power. Although the Saudis lacked the military might to counter the Iraqi threat, it assured its own defense by underwriting one of the biggest, and most complex military buildups in history. It also came through with loans and other financial aid, and persuaded the tight-fisted leaders of Kuwait and the United Arab Emirates to do the same, for key members of the United Nations Security Council, particularly the Soviet Union.

Moreover, the Gulf War forced the traditionally low-key Saudis for the first time to engage in aggressive diplomacy, calling in the favors owed to it by nations throughout the world largely because of the economic relationship. Those like Jordan, which failed to respond as the Saudis expected, paid a high price.

The Saudis have continued a more activist diplomatic role. A prime example came in the precedent-setting Middle East peace conference in Madrid in November 1991. Acting as a personal envoy of King Fahd, Ambassador Prince Bandar was credited with playing a key role in keeping the talks going when it appeared they would collapse. Prior to the historic conference Prince Bandar travelled to Damascus to meet with Syrian President Assad, who assured the prince that Syria would live up to its commitment and attend. But when the three-day opening session of the conference ended in a volley of acrimonious charges and counter-charges between Israel and Syria, Syria was on the verge of bolting without moving on to the vital second stage of direct talks with Israel. Bandar reportedly persuaded the Syrian Foreign Minister to go to the table with the obstinate Israelis. To ensure progress, King Fahd followed up by calling President Assad.

In addition, when the Palestinians and Jordanians said that regardless of Syria's decision, they wanted to proceed to the direct talks with Israel, the Saudis said they would back them in their stand.

Saudi Efforts to Convert Oil into Political Power

During the War, Saudi Arabia helped bring down skyrocketing oil prices by stepping up production to levels few people thought were possible. In the recession that plagued most nations' economies following the War, the Saudis maintained high production levels so as to keep oil prices stable. This stems from the Saudi's "balance of interests" policy which holds that too high of an oil price, though good for short-term windfalls, ultimately will hurt the Saudi economy by dragging down, or even threatening the world economy.

However, when the European Community (EC) contemplated altering this balance by a $3 barrel increase in the oil tax, the Saudis flexed their economic muscle. Saudi Oil Minister Hisham Nazir said the tax was designed to finance the EC's own largesse at a time that the twelve EC governments earned $210 billion from oil taxes in 1991. Saudi sources indicated they were willing to limit oil production and let prices rise $3 a barrel. Just the mention of it caused the Dow Jones average to drop twenty-two points, as U.S. dependence on foreign oil was placed at 40 percent. Saudi Arabia, the world's largest oil exporter, provided one of every ten barrels of oil consumed in the United States in 1991.

One important payoff for Saudi Arabia is that it increased its share of the world's oil production from 25 to 35 percent. It continues to diversify its economy through "downstream" oil and petrochemical industries, and through construction. Perhaps the most important result of the post-War order is not that Saudi Arabia has increased its productive capacity, but that it is grappling with the difficult issues of accommodating the needs of its domestic population, while at the same time, learning how to transform its economic might into political influence.

While some experts are predicting that the twenty-first century will belong to Europe, others are saying it will be wise to keep an eye on Saudi Arabia.

CHAPTER 2

Saudi Arabia and the September 11, 2001, Attacks on America

Muslims Must Retaliate Against American Aggression in Saudi Arabia

By Osama bin Laden et al.

Born in 1957 to a Syrian mother and a Yemenese father, Osama bin Laden was one of about fifty sons and daughters who were heirs to a family fortune earned from a Saudi construction company. Bin Laden was raised a devout Muslim and exhibited a tendency to support conservative Islamic movements while studying management and economics at King Abdul Aziz University in Jeddah, Saudi Arabia. Bin Laden became active in politics after the Soviet invasion of Afghanistan in 1979, and in the mid-1980s he established an organization in Afghanistan that recruited soldiers for the jihad, or holy war, against the Soviets. When the Afghan war ended in 1989, bin Laden returned to Saudi Arabia to work in the family construction business, but he was quickly repoliticized when the Gulf War between the United States and Iraq began in 1990. Bin Laden was angered when the Saudi monarch invited an "infidel" army to protect the Muslim holy lands in Saudi Arabia instead of relying on Muslim veterans from the Afghan war. Throughout the 1990s, bin Laden intensified his efforts to expel the American army from Saudi Arabia by force—efforts that culminated with the terrorist attacks in New York and Washington, D.C., on September 11, 2001. In the following excerpt, bin Laden issues a fatwa, or religious order, dated February 23, 1998, commanding Muslims to kill Americans and their allies until

*they have withdrawn their army from Saudi Arabia and ceased attacking
other Islamic countries.*

Praise be to God, who revealed the Book, controls the clouds, de-
feats factionalism, and says in His Book, "But when the forbidden months are past, then fight and slay the pagans wherever ye find
them, seize them, beleaguer them, and lie in wait for them in every
stratagem of war." And peace be upon our Prophet, Muhammad Bin-
'Abdallah, who said I have been sent with the sword between my
hands to ensure that no one but God is worshipped, God who put my
livelihood under the shadow of my spear and who inflicts humiliation
and scorn on those who disobey my orders. The Arabian Peninsula has
never—since God made it flat, created its desert, and encircled it with
seas—been stormed by any forces like the crusader armies spreading
in it like locusts, eating its riches and wiping out its plantations. All
this is happening at a time in which nations are attacking Muslims like
people fighting over a plate of food. In the light of the grave situation
and the lack of support, we and you are obliged to discuss current
events, and we should all agree on how to settle the matter.

No one argues today about three facts that are known to everyone;
we will list them, in order to remind everyone:

First, since 1990 the United States has been occupying the lands
of Islam in the holiest of places, the Arabian Peninsula, plundering
its riches, dictating to its rulers, humiliating its people, terrorizing its
neighbors, and turning its bases in the Peninsula into a spearhead
through which to fight the neighboring Muslim peoples.

If some people have in the past argued about the fact of the occupation, all the people of the Peninsula have now acknowledged it.

The best proof of this is the Americans' continuing aggression
against the Iraqi people using the Peninsula as a staging post, even
though all its rulers are against their territories being used to that end,
but they are helpless. Second, despite the great devastation inflicted on
the Iraqi people by the crusader-Zionist alliance, and despite the huge
number of those killed, which has exceeded 1 million, despite all this,
the Americans are once again trying to repeat the horrific massacres,
as though they are not content with the protracted blockade imposed
after the ferocious [Gulf] war or the fragmentation and devastation.

So here they come to annihilate what is left of this people and to
humiliate their Muslim neighbors.

Third, if the Americans' aims behind these wars are religious and
economic, the aim is also to serve the Jews' petty state and divert attention from its occupation of Jerusalem and murder of Muslims there.

The best proof of this is their eagerness to destroy Iraq, the strongest neighboring Arab state, and their endeavor to fragment all the states of the region such as Iraq, Saudi Arabia, Egypt, and Sudan into paper statelets and through their disunion and weakness to guarantee Israel's survival and the continuation of the brutal crusade occupation of the Peninsula.

All these crimes and sins committed by the Americans are a clear declaration of war on God, his messenger, and Muslims. And ulema [the body of mullahs, Islamic religious scholars] have throughout Islamic history unanimously agreed that the jihad [holy war] is an individual duty if the enemy destroys the Muslim countries. . . .

On that basis, and in compliance with God's order, we issue the following fatwa to all Muslims:

The ruling to kill the Americans and their allies—civilians and military—is an individual duty for every Muslim who can do it in any country in which it is possible to do it, in order to liberate the al-Aqsa Mosque and the holy mosque [Mecca] from their grip, and in order for their armies to move out of all the lands of Islam, defeated and unable to threaten any Muslim. This is in accordance with the words of Almighty God, "and fight the pagans all together as they fight you all together," and "fight them until there is no more tumult or oppression, and there prevail justice and faith in God."

This is in addition to the words of Almighty God, "and why should ye not fight in the cause of God and of those who, being weak, are ill-treated and oppressed—women and children, whose cry is 'Our Lord, rescue us from this town, whose people are oppressors; and raise for us from thee one who will help!'"

We—with God's help—call on every Muslim who believes in God and wishes to be rewarded to comply with God's order to kill the Americans and plunder their money wherever and whenever they find it. We also call on Muslim ulema, leaders, youths, and soldiers to launch the raid on Satan's U.S. troops and the devil's supporters allying with them, and to displace those who are behind them so that they may learn a lesson.

Almighty God said, "O ye who believe, give your response to God and His Apostle, when He calleth you to that which will give you life. And know that God cometh between a man and his heart, and that it is He to whom ye shall all be gathered."

Almighty God also says, "O ye who believe, what is the matter with you, that when ye are asked to go forth in the cause of God, ye cling so heavily to the earth! Do ye prefer the life of this world to the hereafter? But little is the comfort of this life, as compared with the hereafter. . . .

Almighty God also says, "So lose no heart, nor fall into despair. For ye must gain mastery if ye are true in faith."

Terrorism Is Contrary to the Tenets of Islam

By Shaykh Abdul Aziz Alush-Shaykh

Shaykh Abdul Aziz Alush-Shaykh is the head of the Saudi commission of senior Islamic scholars and the grand mufti, or highest religious official, of Saudi Arabia. The Shaykh assumed his office in 2000 after the death of Shaykh abd Al-Aziz Bin Baz, a man who advocated a very strict interpretation of the shariah *(Islamic law). In a surprise move in May 2001, Shaykh Abdul Aziz condemned the use of suicide attacks as a means to conduct jihad, or holy war, signaling a potential shift in the conservative orientation of Saudi religious authorities. In the passage that follows, the Shaykh issues a fatwa, or religious order, condemning the terrorist attacks against the United States on September 11, 2001. The Shaykh cites the Koran and the writings of the prophet Muhammad to support his ruling, which condemns not only the attacks against the United States, but also condemns taking hostages or killing innocent people for any cause.*

All praise is due to the Lord of the Worlds, the successful end is for the pious, and prayers and peace be upon the noblest of Prophets and Messengers, and upon his family, and his companions.

To proceed:

Due to abundant questions and enquiries that have been brought to us concerning what happened in the United States of America Sept. 11, 2001, and concerning the *Sharî'ah* (Islamic law) position towards it, and whether the religion of Islâm affirms the likes of these actions or not, I say, seeking aid and assistance from Allâh, the Unique, the Over-Powerer, that Allâh, free is He from all imperfection, has bestowed upon us the favour of this Islâmic religion and has

Shaykh Abdul Aziz Alush-Shaykh, "Fatwa from Grand Mufti of Saudi Arabia on USA Terrorism," www.sunnahonline.com, September 6, 2002.

made it a complete legislation, a perfect and all-inclusive one which is beneficial for all times, places, and all situations, for all individuals and groups of individuals. It invites towards rectification and uprightness and justice and goodness, and also the removal of *Shirk* (paganism, ascribing false partners with Allâh), and evil, oppression, injustice and deceit.

And it is from the greatest of favours of Allâh upon us, we the Muslims, that He has guided us to this religion, and has made us its followers and helpers. Hence, a Muslim is cultivated by the legislation of Allâh, a follower of the *Sunnah* (the way) of the Messenger of Allâh, and one who remains upright and steadfast upon this religion—he is the one who will be the saved Muslim in this life and the Hereafter.

As for what has happened in the United States of America of very dangerous occurrences, on account of which thousands of souls have passed away, on account of actions that the Islâmic *Sharî'ah* does not sanction, and which are not from this religion, and these actions do not agree with the spirit and foundations of the legislation from numerous angles:

Verily, Allâh, free is He from all imperfections, has commanded justice, and is based upon justice that the Heavens and the Earth stand, and it is on account of this justice that the Messengers were sent and the Books were revealed. Allâh the free from all imperfections, said, "Verily, Allâh commands with justice and benevolence, and the giving of near relatives, (in charity) and He forbids from obscene and evil deeds, and oppression. He cautions you, that perchance you may remember."

And He also says, "We have indeed sent Messengers with clear proofs and we have revealed with them, the Book and the Balance, so that the people may abide by justice."

And Allâh has judged and decreed that one soul cannot bear the burden of another soul, this due to the perfection of Allâh's justice, free is He from imperfection. He said, "And no bearer of burdens will bear the burden of another."

Indeed, Allâh, free is He from all imperfections, has forbidden oppression on His own self, and He has also declared it forbidden for his servants, as he said in the *hadîth quadsî*, *"O My servants, indeed I have forbidden oppression upon Myself and I have also made it forbidden amongst yourselves, hence do not oppress each other."*

And this is general for all of the servants of Allâh, both the Muslims amongst them and the Non-Muslim, and it is not permissible for any one of them to be unjust to another, nor for him to oppress him, even if it is in the presence of hate and dislike. Allâh, free is He from all imperfections says, "O you who believe. Be of those who stand up to Al-lâh, as witnesses of justice. And let not the hatred of a people make you swerve away from justice towards them. Verily, be just and that is closer to piety." Hence, even hatred and dislike do not permit the commission of injustice and oppression, from a legislative point of view.

Based upon what has preceded, it is obligatory for all of us to know—both states and societies, Muslims and Non-Muslims—a number of important matters:

1. That these matters that have taken place in the United States and whatever else is of the nature of plane hijackings and taking people hostage or killing innocent people, without a just cause, this is nothing but a manifestation of injustice, oppression and tyranny, which the Islâmic *Sharî'ah* does not sanction or accept, rather it is expressly forbidden and it is amongst the greatest of sins.

2. That the Muslim who learns the details of his religion, and who acts upon the Book of Allâh and the Sunnah of His Prophet Muhammad does not allow himself to fall into the likes of these actions, due to what they contain, exposing oneself to the wrath of Allâh, and then what results from them of harms and corruption (upon the earth).

3. It is obligatory upon the Scholars of the Muslim Ummah that they explain the truth concerning the likes of these affairs (i.e. terrorist attacks) and that they make clear to the world at large that the *Sharî'ah* of Allâh and the religion of Islâm does not sanction these types of actions, ever.

4. It is upon the media outlets and whoever is behind them, from amongst those who make accusations against the Muslims and who strive to revile this noble and upright religion, and describe it with that which it is free from, all in order to kindle tribulation and to harm the reputation of Islâm and the Muslims and to separate the hearts and constrict the chests—it is obligatory upon them to restrain from this misguidance and to realise that every sane and just person knows of the details of Islâm. The just man knows that it is not possible for him to describe it with these descriptions, and that he cannot make these types of accusations against it, this is because on account of the passing of history, the nations have not known the followers of this religion, and its adherents except to be those who fulfil their rights (due to others) and their absence of injustice and oppression.

And what has preceded is in explanation of the truth and to remove any confusion. And I ask Allâh that he inspire us with that which contains our guidance, that he guides us to the ways of Islâm, and that He strengthens His religion and makes high His word. Indeed He is the Most Kind, the Most Generous. Prayers and peace be upon our Prophet Muhammad, and upon his family and all his companions.

Saudi-American Relations Led to the September 11 Attacks

By Michael T. Klare

Michael T. Klare is a professor of peace and world security studies at the University of Massachusetts–Amherst and a defense correspondent for The Nation. *In the following selection, Klare argues that the conflict between Osama bin Laden's terrorist organization and the United States is not simply a result of ideological differences, nor is it a "backlash against American villainy" in the Middle East. Instead, Klare asserts that the origins of the war on terror are traceable to America's close relationship with Saudi Arabia, which began in the closing months of World War II. At the time, former American president Franklin D. Roosevelt agreed to protect the Saudi kingdom from external threats in exchange for privileged access to its vast oil reserves. This agreement forced subsequent administrations to increase American military involvement in the Persian Gulf. America's increased military presence in the Persian Gulf prompted bin Laden to intensify his efforts to remove U.S. forces from Saudi Arabia by attacking American military personnel and civilians, including those in the World Trade Center and the Pentagon on September 11, 2001.*

There are many ways to view the conflict between the United States and Osama bin Laden's terror network: as a contest between Western liberalism and Eastern fanaticism, as suggested by many pundits in the United States; as a struggle between the defenders and the enemies of authentic Islam, as suggested by many in

Michael T. Klare, "The Geopolitics of War," *The Nation*, vol. 273, November 5, 2001, pp. 11, 12, 14, 15. Copyright © 2001 by *The Nation*. Reproduced by permission.

the Muslim world; and as a predictable backlash against American villainy abroad, as suggested by some on the left. But while useful in assessing some dimensions of the conflict, these cultural and political analyses obscure a fundamental reality: that the war in Afghanistan, like most of the wars that preceded it, is firmly rooted in geopolitical competition.

The geopolitical dimensions of the war are somewhat hard to discern because the initial fighting is taking place in Afghanistan, a place of little intrinsic interest to the United States, and because our principal adversary, bin Laden, has no apparent interest in material concerns. But this is deceptive, because the true center of the conflict is Saudi Arabia, not Afghanistan (or Palestine), and because bin Laden's ultimate objectives include the imposition of a new Saudi government, which in turn would control the single most valuable geopolitical prize on the face of the earth: Saudi Arabia's vast oil deposits, representing one-fourth of the world's known petroleum reserves.

To fully appreciate the roots of the war in Afghanistan, it is necessary to travel back in time—specifically, to the final years of World War II, when the US government began to formulate plans for the world it would dominate in the postwar era. As the war drew to a close, the State Department was enjoined by President Roosevelt to devise the policies and institutions that would guarantee US security and prosperity in the coming epoch. This entailed the design and formation of the United Nations, the construction of the Bretton Woods world financial institutions and, most significant in the current context, the procurement of adequate oil supplies.

American strategists considered access to oil to be especially important because it was an essential factor in the Allied victory over the Axis powers. Although the nuclear strikes on Hiroshima and Nagasaki ended the war, it was oil that fueled the armies that brought Germany and Japan to their knees. Oil powered the vast numbers of ships, tanks and aircraft that endowed Allied forces with a decisive edge over their adversaries, which lacked access to reliable sources of petroleum. It was widely assumed, therefore, that access to large supplies of oil would be critical to US success in any future conflicts.

Oil and American-Saudi Relations

Where would this oil come from? During World Wars I and II, the United States was able to obtain sufficient oil for its own and its allies' needs from deposits in the American Southwest and from Mexico and Venezuela. But most US analysts believed that these supplies would be insufficient to meet American and European requirements in the postwar era. As a result, the State Department initiated an intensive study to identify other sources of petroleum. This effort, led by the department's economic adviser, Herbert Feis, concluded that only one location could provide the needed petroleum. "In all surveys of the situation," Feis noted (in a statement quoted by Daniel Yergin in *The Prize*), "the pencil came to an awed pause at one point and place—the Middle East."

To be more specific, Feis and his associates concluded that the world's most prolific supply of untapped oil was to be found in the Kingdom of Saudi Arabia. But how to get at this oil? At first, the State Department proposed the formation of a government-owned oil firm to acquire concessions in Saudi Arabia and extract the kingdom's reserves. This plan was considered too unwieldy, however, and instead US officials turned this task over to the Arabian American Oil Company (ARAMCO), an alliance of major US oil corporations. But these officials were also worried about the kingdom's long-term stability, so they concluded that the United States would have to assume responsibility for the defense of Saudi Arabia. In one of the most extraordinary occurrences in modern American history, President Roosevelt met with King Abd al-Aziz Ibn Saud, the founder of the modern Saudi regime, on a US warship in the Suez Canal following the February 1945 conference in Yalta. Although details of the meeting have never been made public, it is widely believed that Roosevelt gave the King a promise of US protection in return for privileged American access to Saudi oil—an arrangement that remains in full effect today and constitutes the essential core of the US-Saudi relationship.

This relationship has provided enormous benefits to both sides. The United States has enjoyed preferred access to Saudi petroleum reserves, obtaining about one-sixth of its crude-oil imports from the kingdom. ARAMCO and its US partners have reaped immense profits from their operations in Saudi Arabia and from the distribution of Saudi oil worldwide. (Although ARAMCO's Saudi holdings were nationalized by the Saudi government in 1976, the company continues to manage Saudi oil production and to market its petroleum products abroad.) Saudi Arabia also buys about $6–10 billion worth of goods per year from US companies. The Saudi royal family, for its part, has become immensely wealthy and, because of continued US protection, has remained safe from external and internal attack.

But this extraordinary partnership has also produced a number of unintended consequences, and it is these effects that concern us here. To protect the Saudi regime against its external enemies, the United States has steadily expanded its military presence in the region, eventually deploying thousands of troops in the kingdom. Similarly, to protect the royal family against its internal enemies, US personnel have become deeply involved in the regime's internal security apparatus. At the same time, the vast and highly conspicuous accumulation of wealth by the royal family has alienated it from the larger Saudi population and led to charges of systemic corruption. In response, the regime has outlawed all forms of political debate in the kingdom (there is no parliament, no free speech, no political party, no right of assembly) and used its US-trained security forces to quash overt expressions of dissent. All these effects have generated covert opposition to the regime and occasional acts of violence—and it is from this underground milieu that Osama bin Laden has drawn his inspiration and many of his top lieutenants.

The Carter Doctrine and the US Military Presence in Saudi Arabia

The US military presence in Saudi Arabia steadily increased over the years. Initially, from 1945 to 1972, Washington delegated the primary defense responsibility to Britain, long the dominant power in the region. When Britain withdrew its forces from "East of Suez" in 1971, the United States assumed a more direct role, deploying military advisers in the kingdom and providing Saudi Arabia with a vast arsenal of US weapons. Some of these arms and advisory programs were aimed at external defense, but the Defense Department also played a central role in organizing, equipping, training and managing the Saudi Arabian National Guard (SANG), the regime's internal security force.

American military involvement in the kingdom reached a new level in 1979, when three things happened: The Soviet Union invaded Afghanistan, the Shah of Iran was overthrown by anti-government forces and Islamic militants staged a brief rebellion in Mecca. In response, President Jimmy Carter issued a new formulation of US policy: Any move by a hostile power to gain control of the Persian Gulf area would be regarded "as an assault on the vital interests of the United States of America" and would be resisted "by any means necessary, including military force." This statement, now known as the "Carter Doctrine," has governed US strategy in the gulf ever since.

To implement the new doctrine, Carter established the Rapid Deployment Force, a collection of combat forces based in the United States but available for deployment to the Persian Gulf. (The RDF was later folded into the US Central Command, which now conducts all US military operations in the region.) Carter also deployed US warships in the gulf and arranged for the periodic utilization by American forces of military bases in Bahrain, Diego Garcia (a British-controlled island in the Indian Ocean), Oman and Saudi Arabia—all of which were employed during the 1990–91 Gulf War and are again being used today. Believing, moreover, that the Soviet presence in Afghanistan represented a threat to US dominance in the gulf, Carter authorized the initiation of covert operations to undermine the Soviet-backed regime there. (It is important to note that the Saudi regime was deeply involved in this effort, providing much of the funding for the anti-Soviet rebellion and allowing its citizens, including Osama bin Laden, to participate in the war effort as combatants and fundraisers.) And to protect the Saudi royal family, Carter increased US involvement in the kingdom's internal security operations.

The Negative Consequences of American Bases in Saudi Arabia

President Reagan accelerated Carter's overt military moves and greatly increased covert US support for the anti-Soviet mujahedeen in Afghanistan. (Eventually, some $3 billion worth of arms were given to the mujahedeen.) Reagan also issued an important codicil to the Carter Doctrine: The United States would not allow the Saudi regime to be overthrown by internal dissidents, as occurred in Iran. "We will not permit [Saudi Arabia] to be an Iran," he told reporters in 1981.

Then came the Persian Gulf War. When Iraqi forces invaded Kuwait on August 2, 1990, President Bush the elder was principally concerned about the threat to Saudi Arabia, not Kuwait. At a meeting at Camp David on August 4, he determined that the United States must take immediate military action to defend the Saudi kingdom against possible Iraqi attack. To allow for a successful defense of the kingdom, Bush sent his Secretary of Defense, Dick Cheney, to Riyadh to persuade the royal family to allow the deployment of US ground forces on Saudi soil and the use of Saudi bases for airstrikes against Iraq.

The subsequent unfolding of Operation Desert Storm does not need to be retold here. What is important to note is that the large US military presence in Saudi Arabia was never fully withdrawn after the end of the fighting in Kuwait. American aircraft continue to fly from bases in Saudi Arabia as part of the enforcement mechanism of the "no-fly zone" over southern Iraq (intended to prevent the Iraqis from using this airspace to attack Shiite rebels in the Basra area or to support a new invasion of Kuwait). American aircraft also participate in the multinational effort to enforce the continuing economic sanctions on Iraq.

President Clinton further strengthened the US position in the gulf, expanding American basing facilities there and enhancing the ability to rapidly move US-based forces to the region. Clinton also sought to expand US influence in the Caspian Sea basin, an energy-rich area just to the north of the Persian Gulf.

Many consequences have flowed from all this. The sanctions on Iraq have caused immense suffering for the Iraqi population, while the regular bombing of military facilities produces a mounting toll of Iraqi civilian deaths. Meanwhile, the United States has failed to take any action to curb Israeli violence against the Palestinians. It is these concerns that have prompted many young Muslims to join bin Laden's forces. Bin Laden himself, however, is most concerned about Saudi Arabia. Ever since the end of the Gulf War, he has focused his efforts on achieving two overarching goals: the expulsion of the American "infidels" from Saudi Arabia (the heart of the Muslim holy land) and the overthrow of the current Saudi regime and its replacement with one more attuned to his fundamentalist Islamic beliefs.

Both of these goals put bin Laden in direct conflict with the United States. It is this reality, more than any other, that explains the terrorist strikes on US military personnel and facilities in the Middle East, and key symbols of American power in New York and Washington.

The Afghan war did not begin on September 11, 2001. As far as we can tell, it began in 1993 with the first attack on the World Trade Center. This was succeeded in 1995 with an attack on the SANG headquarters in Riyadh, and in 1996 with the explosion at the Khobar Towers outside of Dhahran. Then followed the 1998 bombings of the US embassies in Kenya and Tanzania, and the more recent attack on the USS Cole. All these events, like the World Trade Center/Pentagon assaults, are consistent with a long-term strategy to erode US determination to maintain its alliance with the Saudi regime—and thus, in the final analysis, to destroy the 1945 compact forged by President Roosevelt and King Abd al-Aziz Ibn Saud.

The Future of Saudi-American Relations

In fighting against these efforts, the United States is acting, in the first instance, to protect itself, its citizens and its military personnel from terrorist violence. At the same time, however, Washington is also shoring up its strategic position in the Persian Gulf. With bin Laden out of the way, Iran suffering from internal political turmoil and Saddam Hussein immobilized by unrelenting American airstrikes, the dominant US position in the gulf will be assured for some time to come. (Washington's one big worry is that the Saudi monarchy will face increasing internal opposition because of its close association with the United States; it is for this reason that the Bush Administration has not leaned too hard on the regime to permit US forces to use Saudi bases for attacks on Afghanistan and to freeze the funds of Saudi charities linked to Osama bin Laden.)

For both sides, then, this conflict has important geopolitical dimensions. A Saudi regime controlled by Osama bin Laden could be expected to sever all ties with US oil companies and to adopt new policies regarding the production of oil and the distribution of the country's oil wealth—moves that would have potentially devastating consequences for the US, and indeed the world, economy. The United States, of course, is fighting to prevent this from happening.

As the conflict unfolds, we are unlikely to hear any of this from the key figures involved. In seeking to mobilize public support for his campaign against the terrorists, President Bush will never acknowledge that conventional geopolitics plays a role in US policy. Osama bin Laden, for his part, is equally reluctant to speak in such terms. But the fact remains that this war, like the Gulf War before it, derives from a powerful geopolitical contest.

It will be very difficult, in the current political environment, to probe too deeply into these matters. Bin Laden and his associates have caused massive injury to the United States, and the prevention of further such attacks is, understandably, the nation's top priority. When conditions permit, however, a serious review of US policy in the Persian Gulf will be in order. Among the many questions that might legitimately be asked at this point is whether long-term US interests would not best be served by encouraging the democratization of Saudi Arabia. Surely, if more Saudi citizens are permitted to participate in open political dialogue, fewer will be attracted to the violent, anti-American dogma of Osama bin Laden.

Wahhabi Islam in Saudi Arabia Inspired the Attacks on America

By Stephen Schwartz

In the nineteenth century, the first monarch of the Al Saud dynasty, Ibn Saud, made a pact with a fringe Islamic sect called the Wahhabis, which was named for its founder Ibn Abdul Wahhab. The Wahhabis were instrumental in help- ing the Al Saud family conquer the Arabian Peninsula and in establishing the state of Saudi Arabia in 1932. Stephen Schwartz, a writer whose recently pub- lished works include Intellectuals and Assassins, *discusses the spread of Wah- habism in the selection below. According to Schwartz, the fundamentalist in- terpretation of Islam proselytized by the Wahhabis is what inspired Osama bin Laden and his organization to attack the World Trade Center and Penta- gon on September 11, 2001. Schwartz also asserts that the alliance between the Saudi state and the Wahhabi clergy encouraged the spread of the ideolo- gies that motivated bin Laden and other radical Islamic groups.*

The first thing to do when trying to understand 'Islamic suicide bombers' is to forget the clichés about the Muslim taste for mar- tyrdom. It does exist, of course, but the desire for paradise is not a safe guide to what motivated the appalling suicide attacks on New York and Washington on Sept. 11, 2001. Throughout history, politi- cal extremists of all faiths have willingly given up their lives simply in the belief that by doing so, whether in bombings or in other forms of terror, they would change the course of history, or at least win an advantage for their cause. Tamils are not Muslims, but they blow

Stephen Schwartz, "Ground Zero and the Saudi Connection," *The Spectator*, September 22, 2001, pp. 12–13. Copyright © 2001 by *The Spectator*. Reproduced by permission.

themselves up in their war on the government of Sri Lanka; Japanese kamikaze pilots in the second world war were not Muslims, but they flew their fighters into US aircraft carriers.

The Islamofascist ideology of Osama bin Laden and those closest to him, such as the Egyptian and Algerian 'Islamic Groups', is no more intrinsically linked to Islam or Islamic civilisation than Pearl Harbor was to Buddhism, or Ulster terrorists—whatever they may profess—are to Christianity. Serious Christians don't go around killing and maiming the innocent; devout Muslims do not prepare for paradise by hanging out in strip bars and getting drunk, as one of the terrorist pilots was reported to have done.

The attacks of 11 September are simply not compatible with orthodox Muslim theology, which cautions soldiers 'in the way of Allah' to fight their enemies face-to-face, without harming non-combatants, women or children. Most Muslims, not only in America and Britain, but in the world, are clearly law-abiding citizens of their countries—a point stressed by President Bush and other American leaders, much to their credit. Nobody on this side of the water wants a repeat of the lamented 1941 internment of Japanese Americans.

Still, the numerical preponderance of Muslims as perpetrators of these ghastly incidents is no coincidence. So we have to ask ourselves what has made these men into the monsters they are? What has so galvanised violent tendencies in the world's second-largest religion (and, in America, the fastest growing faith)? Can it really flow from a quarrel over a bit of land in the Middle East?

The Origins of Islamic Extremism

For Westerners, it seems natural to look for answers in the distant past, beginning with the Crusades. But if you ask educated, pious, traditional but forward-looking Muslims what has driven their *umma*, or global community, in this direction, many of them will answer you with one word: Wahhabism. This is a strain of Islam that emerged not at the time of the Crusades, nor even at the time of the anti-Turkish wars of the 17th century, but less than two centuries ago. It is violent, it is intolerant, and it is fanatical beyond measure. It originated in Arabia, and it is the official theology of the Gulf states. Wahhabism is the most extreme form of Islamic fundamentalism, and its followers are called Wahhabis.

Not all Muslims are suicide bombers, but all Muslim suicide bombers are Wahhabis—except, perhaps, for some disciples of atheist leftists posing as Muslims in the interests of personal power, such as Yasser Arafat or Saddam Hussein. Wahhabism is the Islamic equivalent of the most extreme Protestant sectarianism. It is puritan, demanding punishment for those who enjoy any form of music except the drum, and severe punishment up to death for drinking or sexual transgressions. It condemns as unbelievers those who do not pray, a view that never previously existed in mainstream Islam.

It is stripped-down Islam, calling for simple, short prayers, undecorated mosques, and the uprooting of gravestones (since decorated mosques and graveyards tend themselves to veneration, which is idolatry in the Wahhabi mind). Wahhabis do not even permit the name of the Prophet Mohammed to be inscribed in mosques, nor do they allow his birthday to be celebrated. Above all, they hate ostentatious spirituality, much as Protestants detest the veneration of miracles and saints in the Roman Church.

Ibn Abdul Wahhab (1703–92), the founder of this totalitarian Islamism, was born in Uyaynah, in the part of Arabia known as Nejd, where Riyadh is today, and which the Prophet himself notably warned would be a source of corruption and confusion. . . . From the beginning of Wahhab's dispensation, in the late 18th century his cult was associated with the mass murder of all who opposed it. For example, the Wahhabis fell upon the city of Qarbala in 1801 and killed 2,000 ordinary citizens in the streets and markets.

In the 19th century, Wahhabism took the form of Arab nationalism *v.* the Turks. The founder of the Saudi kingdom, Ibn Saud, established Wahhabism as its official creed. Much has been made of the role of the US in 'creating' Osama bin Laden through subsidies to the Afghan mujahedin, but as much or more could be said in reproach of Britain which, three generations before, supported the Wahhabi Arabs in their revolt against the Ottomans. Arab hatred of the Turks fused with Wahhabi ranting against the 'decadence' of Ottoman Islam. The truth is that the Ottoman *khalifa* reigned over a multinational Islamic *umma* in which vast differences in local culture and tradition were tolerated. No such tolerance exists in Wahhabism, which is why the concept of US troops on Saudi soil so inflames bin Laden.

Bin Laden is a Wahhabi. So are the suicide bombers in Israel. So are his Egyptian allies, who exulted as they stabbed foreign tourists to death at Luxor not many years ago, bathing in blood up to their elbows and emitting blasphemous cries of ecstasy. So are the Algerian Islamist terrorists whose contribution to the purification of the world consisted of murdering people for such sins as running a movie projector or reading secular newspapers. So are the Taleban-style guerrillas in Kashmir who murder Hindus. The Iranians are not Wahhabis, which partially explains their slow but undeniable movement towards moderation and normality after a period of utopian and puritan revivalism. But the Taleban practise a variant of Wahhabism. In the Wahhabi fashion they employ ancient punishments—such as execution for moral offences—and they have a primitive and fearful view of women. The same is true of Saudi Arabia's rulers. None of this extremism has been inspired by American fumblings in the world, and it has little to do with the tragedies that have beset Israelis and Palestinians.

The Weaknesses of Wahhabism

But the Wahhabis have two weaknesses of which the West is largely unaware; an Achilles' heel on each foot, so to speak. The first is that the vast majority of Muslims in the world are peaceful people who would prefer the installation of Western democracy in their own countries. They loathe Wahhabism for the same reason any patriarchal culture rejects a violent break with tradition. And that is the point that must be understood: bin Laden and other Wahhabis are not defending Islamic tradition; they represent an ultra-radical break in the direction of a sectarian utopia. Thus, they are best described as Islamofascists, although they have much in common with Bolsheviks.

The Bengali Sufi writer Zeeshan Ali has described the situation touchingly: 'Muslims from Bangladesh in the US, just like any other place in the world, uphold the traditional beliefs of Islam but, due to lack of instruction, keep quiet when their beliefs are attacked by Wahhabis in the US who all of a sudden become "better" Muslims than others. These Wahhabis go even further and accuse their own fathers of heresy, sin and unbelief. And the young children of the immigrants, when they grow up in this country, get exposed only to this one-sided version of Islam and are led to think that this is the only Islam. Naturally a big gap is being created every day that silence is only widening.' The young, divided between tradition and the call of the new, opt for 'Islamic revolution' and commit themselves to their self-destruction, combined with mass murder.

The same influences are brought to bear throughout the ten-million-strong Muslim community in America, as well as those in Europe. In the US, 80 per cent of mosques are estimated by the Sufi Hisham al-Kabbani, born in Lebanon and now living in the US, to be under the control of Wahhabi imams, who preach extremism, and this leads to the other point of vulnerability: Wahhabism is subsidised by Saudi Arabia, even though bin Laden has sworn to destroy the Saudi royal family. The Saudis have played a double game for years, more or less as Stalin did with the West during the second world war. They pretended to be allies in a common struggle against Saddam Hussein while they spread Wahhabi ideology everywhere Muslims are to be found, just as Stalin promoted an 'antifascist' coalition with the US while carrying out espionage and subversion on American territory. The motive was the same: the belief that the West was or is decadent and doomed.

Terrorism and the Saudi Connection

One major question is never asked in American discussions of Arab terrorism: what is the role of Saudi Arabia? The question cannot be asked because American companies depend too much on the continued flow of Saudi oil, while American politicians have become too cosy with the Saudi rulers.

Another reason it is not asked is that to expose the extent of Saudi and Wahhabi influence on American Muslims would deeply compromise many Islamic clerics in the US. But it is the most significant question Americans should be asking themselves today. If we get rid of bin Laden, who do we then have to deal with? The answer was eloquently put by Seyyed Vali Reza Nasr, professor of political science at the University of California at San Diego, and author of an authoritative volume on Islamic extremism in Pakistan, when he said: 'If the US wants to do something about radical Islam, it has to deal with Saudi Arabia. The "rogue states" [Iraq, Libya, etc.] are less important in the radicalisation of Islam than Saudi Arabia. Saudi Arabia is the single most important cause and supporter of radicalisation, ideologisation, and the general fanaticisation of Islam.'

From what we now know, it appears not a single one of the suicide pilots in New York and Washington was Palestinian. They all seem to have been Saudis, citizens of the Gulf states, Egyptian or Algerian. Two are reported to have been the sons of the former second secretary of the Saudi embassy in Washington. They were planted in America long before the outbreak of the latest Palestinian intifada (uprising): in fact, they seem to have begun their conspiracy while the Middle East peace process was in full, if short, bloom. Anti-terror experts and politicians in the West must now consider the Saudi connection.

CHAPTER 3

Tensions and Changes in Saudi Arabian Foreign Relations

American Foreign Policy Cannot Change Saudi Arabia

By Adam Garfinkle

Adam Garfinkle served on the staff of the U.S. Commission on National Security/21st Century, was a senior fellow at the Foreign Policy Research Institute, and is currently the editor of The National Interest. *Garfinkle argues in the following selection that the cultures of the United States and Saudi Arabia are inherently incompatible and that American citizens and policy makers should recognize this fact. While Garfinkle does not argue that the United States should "learn to live" with an Islamic fundamentalist regime in Saudi Arabia, he does assert that it is not the time to press for a change in Saudi society. According to Garfinkle, the United States should adapt its behavior toward Saudi Arabia by recognizing its anti-Western political culture. He also implies that doing so will allow the United States to optimize its strategic and economic interests in the Middle East.*

In the 1960s, R.G. Collingwood wrote, "Every new generation must rewrite history in its own way." Inasmuch as his thinking was suspended somewhere between hope for a science of history and an awareness of its practical limits, philosophers of history have been arguing ever since about what he really meant. But one thing he must have meant is that what interests us about the past is at least partly a function of what bothers us or makes us curious in the present. As Collingwood said, "As far as we can see history as a whole . . . we see it as a continuous development in which every phase consists of

Adam Garfinkle, "Weak Realpolitik: The Vicissitudes of Saudi Bashing," *The National Interest*, Spring 2002, pp. 144–50. Copyright © 2002 by *The National Interest*. Reproduced by permission.

the solution of human problems set by the preceding phase."

Human affairs generally move so ponderously, or in such complicated ways, that contemporaries have trouble seeing "history as a whole", or detecting the phases to which Collingwood pointed. But as a glacier or a tectonic plate may slip to dramatic effect, so sometimes major events rattle us into historical awareness. When they do, it is uncanny how we find ourselves reassessing the significance of dates as symbols of the touching points of historical phases. . . . September 11, 2001, was such an event, so it is worth asking how our historical perceptions may change as a result of it.

To be sure, some movement in our historical awareness may be detected already. Americans have grown intensely interested in the Middle East and Islam in general—and in Saudi Arabia, Saudi Islam, and the U.S.-Saudi relationship in particular. So far, however, relatively recent matters have monopolized our attention, and an abundance of detailed newspaper feature series has contributed to that focus. The seriousness of our historical thinking is also affected by emotion. We Americans are more than just curious, and more than merely bothered, about these Saudi subjects. Some are better described as very, very angry.

For starters, it soon dawned on us that while the targets of initial U.S.-led military operations would be the Al-Qaeda organization nestled in the bosom of the Taliban regime, the real source of the problem lay in our two most tactically significant *allies*: Pakistan and Saudi Arabia. As to the former, we knew that Pakistan's military and intelligence services had created and supported the Taliban, thus providing sanctuary and foot soldiers for mass-casualty terrorism. As to the latter, not only were 15 of the 19 terrorists Saudi nationals, but the open secret that the Saudi regime deflects popular frustration and opposition away from itself and onto the United States and Israel became more widely confessed in public. As Sandy Berger put it once out of office, "the veil has been lifted and the American people see a double game that they're not terribly pleased with." Though silent on whether he had been displeased with it while in office, he continued: "They see a regime that is repressive with respect to the extremists that threaten them, but more than tolerant—indeed, the more we find out, beneficent—to the general movement of extreme Islamists in the region.". . .

Just as recognition of these realities was penetrating minds in and around the Beltway, Saudi behavior fed the growing sense of American disquiet. First, Saudi leaders refused to publicly acknowledge that the United States might use Saudi bases against Al-Qaeda and the Taliban, and for a while it was not clear if the U.S. military would even have unfettered unpublicized use of them. At the same time, the Saudi government raised barriers to U.S. law enforcement agencies' efforts to learn about the Saudi terrorists of September 11. Americans were incredulous at being told by Saudi officials, long after it had become even remotely plausible, that few if any of the terrorists were Saudis but had stolen Saudi passports and identities. When subsequently asked to help U.S. officials in the critical task of "following the money" [to Saudi terrorists], Saudi officials at first denied, *pace* Mr. Berger, that any public or private Saudi money had financed any terrorist organization. This raised the question of whether the Saudis were lying, which would have been bad, or whether they were clueless as to what was going on under their noses, which would have been worse. *The New Republic* bluntly summed up the emerging conclusion: "In fact our Arab 'coalition partners'—particularly Saudi Arabia—are actively sabotaging our efforts to identify the wider terrorist international, made up in large part, of course, of their citizens."

Before long, too, recognition of the inadvertent but unmistakable Saudi complicity in September 11 begged the reinterpretation of older data into something of a pattern. The Saudis had impeded the U.S. investigation into the Riyadh and Khobar Towers bombings that killed 23 American soldiers in November 1995 and June 1996. Saudi Arabia is one of the few countries that has refused to participate in a Federal Aviation Administration (FAA)-run airplane manifest agreement that lets U.S. officials know who is arriving into the United States from abroad. The Saudis have at times been unhelpful to sensitive U.S. Arab-Israeli diplomacy, actively dissuading Yasir Arafat during and after the summer 2000 Camp David summit, for example, from accepting compromises over Jerusalem that are a *sine qua non* for a settlement.

More pointedly with regard to Al-Qaeda and company, the Saudis refused to take Osama bin Laden into custody in 1996 when the Sudanese government offered, with American encouragement and support, to deliver him there. As egregious, in April 1995 the Federal Bureau of Investigation (FBI) learned that Imad Mughniyah was on a flight from Khartoum to Beirut that was scheduled to stop in Jeddah, Saudi Arabia. FBI agents rushed to Jeddah to apprehend Mughniyah, who was responsible for the 1985 hijacking of TWA flight 847, during which a U.S. Navy diver was murdered in cold blood, and for the October 1983 bombing of the U.S. Marine complex in Lebanon. But the Saudis refused to let the plane land. (Mughniyah went on to become an important liaison between Hizballah and Al-Qaeda, and is even now helping to host escaped Al-Qaeda terrorists in Lebanon.)

The Saudi Position on American Foreign Policy

As all of this history was being revived, reviewed and discussed, together with post-September 11 developments themselves, the Saudis shouted foul. They claimed, most pointedly, that a conspiracy was being mounted against them by the American media, asserting that this was because so many Jews occupy high positions in that media. Very much related, the Saudis sought to excuse their own reticence to help the United States by alleging, in the person of Crown Prince Abdallah himself on January 28, 2002, that Saudi reluctance flowed from justifiable anger throughout the Arab world over America's "absolute" support for Israel.

Now, Saudi attitudes toward Palestine and Israel, and toward Jews in the American media, may seem like side points considering all the other things that have impinged on U.S. and Saudi interests since September 11. But they are not. The Saudi leadership's approach to Palestine helps define its predicament, stuck as it is between the demands of its own society and its need for friendship and protection from the United States. Moreover, this predicament has been, and will remain, a central and uncomfortable fact in the American war on terrorism.

The Origin of American and Saudi Disagreement

U.S.-Saudi disagreement over Palestinian-Israeli diplomacy had passed through a dramatic stage in the weeks just before September 11, and Saudi complaints after September 11 make little sense without an awareness of that drama. To understand either, however, some background is necessary.

While Saudi Arabia has for decades been ritually referred to by Americans and Europeans as "moderate", there has never been anything the least bit moderate about its basic view of Israel. Saudi religious figures and most Saudi citizens see Israel and Zionism in ways indistinguishable from Al-Qaeda or the Iranian mullahs at their worst (which they frequently are). They accept unquestioningly a passion-play version of the conflict that is entirely one-sided and, given the closed nature of Saudi society, few Saudis have ever even heard any other account. Israel stands irredeemably guilty of "original sin", Palestinians are ever and always mere innocent victims, and no wild Arab press exaggeration—or pure invention—of dark Israeli deeds is too bizarre to be believed. Partly on account of their educational indoctrination, too, many Saudis are avid consumers of anti-Semitism,

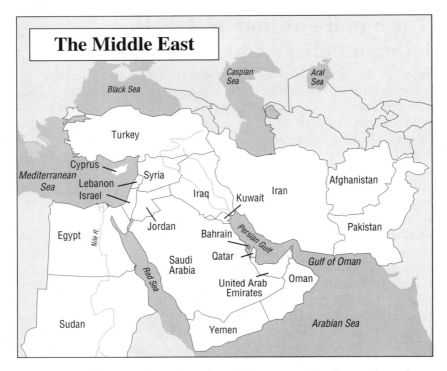

The Middle East

both vintage imported versions from Europe and fresh creations from the pens of contemporary Arabs. It may make at least back-page news in the United States when an official of the Saudi Ministry of Religious Affairs refers to American Jews as "brothers of apes and pigs" and calls on America to "get rid of its Jews", but it is occasion for nods and yawning inside the Kingdom.

In light of this, it seems odd upon a moment's reflection that the Saudi political establishment has always supported Yasir Arafat, the leader and symbol of secular Palestinian nationalism, rather than Islamist alternatives, like Hamas, whose religious-based views are closer to those of Saudi clergy and society. That it has done so illustrates how the Saudi internal dilemma projects itself onto Saudi diplomacy. To be saddled with the political leadership of a weak state means to be simultaneously pragmatic in private and ideologically spotless in public. While the royal family would probably accept any settlement over Palestine that would satisfy Arafat and the nationalists, the Kingdom has been very reluctant to take an active public part in any diplomacy that might in the end legitimate Israel's existence, within any borders whatsoever, for fear of the internal reaction it might provoke. . . . For the Saudi leadership, in any event, Arafat is as moderate a figure as it dares to support.

This is why, despite longstanding and obvious differences between U.S. and Israeli views of a settlement, despite Arafat's having visited the Clinton White House more often than any other foreign dignitary, and despite the fact that the U.S. government has provided more financial support to the Palestinian Authority than has the Saudi government, Saudi leaders still say publicly that U.S. policy has been "absolutely, 100 percent" biased toward Israel during the second so-called *intifada* [Palestinian uprising]. Such a view sounds self-evident to most Saudis because it is accompanied by a parallel belief that *any* support for Israel is unjustified because Israel's very existence is illegitimate. During the period of Palestinian-instigated violence in late 2001 and early 2002, most Saudis saw the Israeli state as terrorist and the Palestinians as blameless targets and martyrs.

Whether Crown Prince Abdallah and his court privately hold the same attitude is not clear. But it is clear that, both before September 11 and since, the Saudi government has acted as it has because it is far more afraid of its own domestic shadow than of Washington's glare. It knows that its own internal peril paradoxically gives it enormous strength in its dealings with the United States because as difficult as the Saudi status quo is, serious people in Washington realize that all the available alternatives are worse. . . .

The Futility of "Saudi Bashing"

A combination of new indignities and old resentments coalesced into a crescendo of American criticism of Saudi Arabia after September 11. Senator Carl Levin was the first, on January 15, 2002, to raise the possibility of withdrawing U.S. forces from Saudi soil, but by the time he went public, an attentive audience in Congress, the Pentagon and elsewhere stood ready to applaud his view. Privately, some senior former U.S. officials began saying things only slightly off the record that would have been hard to imagine six months earlier. At the core of these remarks has been advice to speak frankly, at long last, and at the highest level to the Saudis about key matters that divide us. As Brent Scowcroft put it (for the record), "We probably avoid talking about the things that are the real problems between us because it's a very polite relationship. We don't get all that much below the surface." The developing sense is that we should finally [make] the Saudi leadership to understand that they need us more than we need them.

But is that really true, and is there any sense to such a calculation in the first place? Despite all that has happened since September 11, there has been a limit to Saudi bashing, and for good reason. While

some experts believe that the United States does not need Saudi facilities to make war against the Iraqi Ba'ath regime, for example, most
Pentagon officials would rather do with than without those facilities.
Saudi oil still matters greatly to the limping world economy, too, inasmuch as we have neither a serious energy policy in this country nor
yet a ready substitute for Saudi swing production abroad. . . . More
important, if the United States lets loose of the Saudis to sink or swim
as they might, they might actually sink—only to be replaced by a
regime that more resembles the Taliban than, say, the Hashemites in
Amman. What benefit, then—aside from the idle pleasures of rhetor-
ical release, or the scoring of petty political points—is there in bashing them?

There is none. The point of foreign policymaking is not to feel
good but to do well. A useful step in that direction would be to take
up Collingwood's advice in earnest to rewrite our history.

When we recall our lessons as to what was significant between the
end of World War I and the onset of the Great Depression, we have
been used to naming such items as the Washington Naval Conference, Locarno, and the Kellogg-Briand Pact. From the vantage point
of September 11, however, new historical coordinates arise. In the
wizened, windswept autumn of 1924, the Al Saud wrested owner-
ship of the Hejaz from the Hashemites, who had lorded over the holiest places of Islam since the 10th century. With that conquest—which
could have been prevented by a few gunboats and some strong lan-
guage had British policy not been otherwise bent—the basic territo-
rial configuration of what became known in 1932 as the Kingdom of
Saudi Arabia was established. Meanwhile, in the eastern part of the
Kingdom oil was being found in abundance, and by the 1970s money
began rolling into Saudi coffers in amounts that neither traditional
conceptions nor vaults could hold.

The combination—oil riches and the religious legitimacy con-
ferred by control of Mecca and Medina (and of the *hajj* along with
it)—has allowed the Saudi partnership of the Al Saud and the Al
Wahhab to overturn the equilibrium of Islamic civilization that had
existed for nigh on a thousand years. The Wahhabi version of Sunni
Islam is neither traditional nor orthodox. It is a slightly attenuated
fundamentalism that dates only from the end of the 18th century. . . .
As recently as fifty years ago the large majority of Muslims considered Saudi Wahhabism to be exotic, marginal and austere to the point
of neurotic. But an aggressive and very well-funded campaign of
intra-Islamic evangelism has established it as the paragon of Sunni
piety today. This is, in a word, bad; bad for Arabs, for Muslims, and
for everyone else. More than anything, the ascendancy of Wahhabism

within the Islamic world, to a point that is now beyond the control of the Saudi state, is the core source of the terrorist attacks of September 11—and of the way that those attacks have been variously received and understood by Muslims everywhere.

Irreconcilable Differences Between the United States and Saudi Arabia

Once we understand "1924" properly, we are instantly sobered by the new perspective it provides. We see that Saudi society, caught as it is between its origins and the inexorable press of modernity, is an inherent threat to the United States and to its allies, Arab and non-Arab alike; that by its very nature it cannot help but be such a threat. While we can and should try to persuade the Saudi government to help us "follow the money" [to Saudi terrorists] and to do other things manifestly in its own self-interest as well as ours, we will get nowhere trying to persuade Saudis to be what they are not. We may not like the way Saudis think about the non-Islamic world, or what they teach in their schools, or how they define concepts like charity and terrorism. But for American Christians or Jews to demand that they educate their children to become "better" or "more tolerant" Muslims is utterly futile. Next to the apparently unlimited hubris of those who think it so easy to change the political culture of the Muslim world with so-called Middle East Marshall Plans, this presumption—that we have the right to insist on the reform of other peoples' religions—has to rank as the most outrageous American foolishness of the post-September 11 period.

Too many Americans, then, have simultaneously underestimated the Saudi problem and overestimated the potential near-term efficacy of American influence in regard to it. On the one hand, as a matter of first principle, the United States should not "learn to live" with a *Saudi* Arabia in perpetuity. A Wahhabi-inspired country controlling the Hejaz and that much oil wealth will never be desirable from the perspective of either American interests or values. Arabia has not always been Saudi or Wahhabi, and some day it will probably stop being both; should it become prudent for the United States to advance that day, it would be worth considering. On the other hand, we must recognize that this time is not at hand.

An Argument for the Expulsion of American Forces from Saudi Arabia

By Hayder Ali Khan

Saudi-American relations have been a source of serious contention since the Gulf War of 1990–91, when the United States stationed over a half-million troops on Saudi soil in order to remove the Iraqi army from Kuwait and to protect the Saudi kingdom from invasion. After the end of the war, many Muslim scholars, analysts, and clerics argued that the American presence in Saudi Arabia—a presence that remained at six thousand troops as of September 2002—constituted an illegal occupation of Muslim holy lands. Hayder Ali Khan, a regular contributor to the Islamic periodical Khilafah Magazine, *takes this position and argues that the United States exploited the Saudi people and used its bases to purposefully attack other Islamic countries. Khan concludes by calling on all Muslims to work for the expulsion of American forces in the Middle East, as well as any government in an Islamic country that aligns itself with the United States.*

After more than two continuous months of an unjust and destructive war waged by America against the Muslims of Afghanistan, she succeeded in restoring her influence and control over Afghanistan, and overthrew its rulers and uprooted the Islamic orientation from it. Pentagon sources indicate military bases springing up in as many as 13 locations in nine countries neighbouring Afghanistan, substantially extending the network of bases in the region. Altogether, from Bulgaria and Uzbekistan to Turkey, Kuwait and be-

Hayder Ali Khan, "A Shift in Relations Between America and Saudi Arabia," www.khilafah.com, March 2002. Copyright © 2002 by *Khilafah Magazine*. Reproduced by permission.

yond, more than 60,000 U.S. military personnel now live and work at these bases. While these bases make it easier for the United States to project its power, they also increase prospects for renewed attacks on Americans. One such area where the U.S. presence has motivated hostility amongst the local population is the Desert Arab Kingdom of Saudi Arabia. This article looks at the debate that's taking place in Congress and amongst Saudi officials about the United States-Saudi relationship, and the presence of U.S. bases in the region.

Historical Background to Saudi-American Relations

With Iraq's invasion of Kuwait in August 1990, and the big fear that an aggressive and powerful Iraq would come to control more of the world's Oil supply, the Kingdom . . . invited Washington to use its territory as the launching pad for rolling back Baghdad's occupation. Some 700,000 U.S. troops followed. This came as an enormous shock to elements within the Saudi Kingdom. One such element being Osama Bin Laden, who had initially lobbied the Royal Family to organise a popular defence of the Kingdom and raise a force from the Afghan war veterans to fight Iraq. As the U.S. troops began to arrive, Bin Laden openly criticized the Royal Family, lobbying the Saudi Ulema to issue fatwas [religious orders], against Kuffar [the United States] being based in the country.

After the war, Riyadh agreed to maintain some 20,000 U.S. troops on its soil. It also permitted scores of U.S. warplanes and pilots to be based at the Prince Sultan Air Base, where Washington has installed a state-of-the-art command centre that covers virtually the entire Middle East, Gulf and Central Asia regions. Bin Laden's criticism escalated after seeing the U.S. troops remaining, and eventually the continued criticism of the Saudi Royal family annoyed them so much that they revoked his citizenship in 1994. However, the growing criticism and opposition to the Saudi regime . . . did not die away. The Saudi regime rounded up and arrested hundreds of suspected government opponents from Sunni Islamist opposition groups and subjected them and others to torture and ill treatment (according to reports published by Amnesty International in 1994).

In August 1996, Osama Bin Laden had issued his first declaration of Jihad against the Americans whom he said were occupying Saudi Arabia. "The Walls of oppression and humiliation cannot be demolished except in a rain of bullets", the declaration read. In February of 1998, at a meeting in Afghanistan, Al'Qaeda issued a manifesto under aegis of "The International Islamic Front for Jihad against Jews and Crusaders", The manifesto stated: "For more than seven years the US has been occupying the lands of Islam in the holiest of places, the Arabian peninsula, plundering its riches, dictating to its rulers, humiliating its people, terrorizing its neighbours, and turning its bases in the peninsula into a spearhead through which to fight the neighbouring Muslim peoples." The meeting issued a fatwa targeting Americans.

On August 7th 1998, two explosions took place that rocked the U.S., one of which was at the American embassy in Nairobi, the capital of Kenya and the other at the American embassy in Dar-es-Salaam, the capital of Tanzania. Inside the Persian Gulf area itself, attacks on the Khobar Towers Complex (in Saudi Arabia) and the destroyer U.S.S. Cole in Yemen all added to the increasing pressure on the Saudi regime, and its U.S. masters.

More recently, in a series of rulings in September and October 2001, Shaykh Hammoud bin Uqla al-Shu'aybi declared, "Whoever supports and backs the infidels against Muslims is considered an infidel." The Shaykh is from Buraydah, Saudi Arabia, a town north of Riyadh that has been a hot bed of religious opposition to the Royal family for over a decade now. Similar fatawa issued by Shaykh's Al-Wan and Ali Khudayr rule that those supporting the US war against Afghanistan, "by hand, by tongue, or by money", are automatically excommunicated from Islam. Other fatawa refer specifically to the country's rulers as "infidels". These rulings demonstrate a growing rift between the House of Saud and elements of the Wahhabi sect establishment. They indicate that cracks are emerging in the 256-year illegal pact between the House of Saud and the followers of Muhammad bin 'Abd al-Wahhab (1703–1793).

American and Saudi Interests in the Persian Gulf

In the debate about the U.S.-Saudi relationship, there are growing indications in Congress and reportedly among Saudi officials that a reduction of American military forces in Saudi Arabia is politically inevitable. A force reduction, rather than complete withdrawal, is likely as America assesses her interests. It is in this light that we must understand the recent comments issued by Riyadh. "It is the military presence the Saudi's see as inimical to their interests", said a Riyadh-based diplomat, who spoke on the condition that he is not identified. The conflict appeared to have heated up in the days after the initial comment by the Riyadh-based diplomat, Senator Carl Levin, chairman of the Senate Armed Services Committee, when he suggested that the United States pull its troops out of Saudi Arabia. On the heels of Levin's remarks, an anonymous Saudi official told the *Washington Post* that the U.S. would be asked to leave because it has "overstayed its welcome." Judging by the media coverage, much of the U.S. and international political establishment was taken aback to learn that Saudi Arabia is considering asking Washington to withdraw its military presence from the Kingdom. To people who are politically aware and understand the international situation and have political experience, the story comes as little surprise. In 1997, a group affiliated with the Council on Foreign Relations, and with General Joseph P. Hoar, former Commander in Chief of the United States Central Command, as co-chairman, recommended reassessment of the configuration of American forces in Saudi Arabia and cautioned against maintaining a visible, permanent presence, since that presence can be readily exploited by enemies of the U.S. to inflame Arab sentiments against the Saudi government and the United States. As Charles W. Freeman, a former U.S. ambassador and frequent visitor to Riyadh, told the *Washington Post* recently, "For the first time since 1973, we actually have a situation in which the United States is so unpopular among the (Saudi) public that the Royal family now thinks its security is best served by publicly distancing itself from the United States." Hence we can see clearly, under the circumstances, the co-operation with the United States, once considered to be a military guarantee for the Saudi regime, is now, being seen as a source of political weakness by Riyadh. Riyadh certainly does not want to be "used" in a potential operation . . . against Iraq for fear of a mass uprising within the country, which is already simmering with discontent.

It is clear to see for any observer, that while the Saudi's benefit from American military protection, their own interests, and nothing else drive the United States presence in the region. The U.S. is a Capitalist nation, and hence bases all its actions on the basis of expediency. America's military strategy and interest in the Persian Gulf has always been as much about denying control of oil to enemies . . . as assuring the flow of oil to the West. As well, its occupation of Saudi Arabia after the Gulf War in 1991, provided the U.S. with strategic "depth" in its ability to use Saudi territories and airspace at will to launch attacks against what it now dubs "axis of evil" states. From the reality, there is no other country in the region where the U.S. forces can be deployed at such an extent. Both Riyadh and Washington view the alliance as necessary to preserve regional stability. Also, Washington has always had a close military and intelligence relationship with Riyadh, which has bought more than $50 billion in U.S. arms and construction contracts over the past 20 years with the hundreds of billions of dollars it has earned as the world's biggest oil exporter. Hence it should be understood that the U.S. and the Saudi monarchy need each other and that there aren't any alternatives to each other at the present time. Any harm to Saudi rule would be harmful to American interests. The U.S. is simply protecting its strategic and economic interests by entertaining the thought of altering policy in the Gulf.

After the attacks on Afghanistan, the U.S. senses that its ally, the Saudi monarchy, is weakened politically at home, and is suffering from a waning of popularity. The fact that the Saudi's are seen to have proposed a withdrawal of U.S. troops will add to the credibility of interim leader Crown Prince Abdullah. . . . Abdullah is supported within Saudi Arabia by the young, educated Saudi's because he has not been tainted by scandals. The Islamists also find Abdullah relatively more acceptable for the same reasons as well as for his moderate attitude towards them. So, a U.S. withdrawal, albeit limited, will strengthen the Saudi monarchy somewhat at home, as the opposition's primary demand was that the Americans should leave the "Holy Lands".

The Expulsion of the American Army from Muslim Countries

America deals with the Islamic lands as if they are her own farms. She deals with the rulers of the Muslims as her servants, even as her slaves.

The destruction of the Islamic orientated regime in Afghanistan is not the first aggression of America against the Islamic Ummah. Recently, she hit Iraq and she has laid siege to it since then. She also hit Libya and laid siege to it. She helped the Jews to steal Palestine and to expel its people and she continues to help them. She occupies Saudi Arabia and imposes upon the Gulf her hegemony so that she plunders the Oil and the wealth from their treasuries.

America is the true enemy to the Islamic Ummah. Her allies who share with her in the aggression against the Islamic Ummah or who support her in this aggression, like the English and the French and others, are true enemies to the Islamic Ummah.

It is incorrect to treat the enemy as a friend. It is only the fool who treats the enemy as a friend. And the result of doing so will be evil. . . .

Our rulers [in Muslim countries] should treat America and those who supported her as an arrogant enemy. The Muslim rulers must abolish any military or political treaties and expel all military forces and close down all their military bases. They must also close down their waters, lands and spaces to entry or passage from any of the enemy states so that it makes it harder for the enemy to launch strikes against Muslim lands. They have also to break off any influence and remove any agent or spy for these states in the Islamic lands such as those existent in Al-Azhar and the American University of Beirut. This position is required from every ruler in the Islamic lands, not only from the ruler of the country that is the target of aggression. This is because Muslims are one single Ummah. The Prophet Muhammad said: "The Muslims are like the body, If one of its members complained, the other members will respond in sleeplessness and fever". So aggression against any Islamic land is considered an aggression against all Muslims.

It may be said that the Muslim rulers will not implement any of these actions. It is therefore a duty upon all Muslims to undertake the work to replace these rulers with the system of Khilafah. It is error and complacency in the obligation to leave in power these puppet, vicious rulers who govern with Kufr [the devil] and implement the policies of America or other Kufr countries. Such a ruler, who has in his control the army, the police, and all the forces and institutions and in whose hand lies the implementation of the laws, the funds of the country, who is occupying the seat of power, It is haram to leave in power such a ruler who is spreading corruption in the land/and protecting the influence of the Americans and their allies, and to distract oneself from that by challenging a little of the Kuffar's influence.

Can the Islamic peoples change their rulers? Yes, definitely. America and its allies will never be able to protect the despicable puppet ruler from his people, particularly when such a ruler is a coward who protects his own interests and the interests of a foreign disbelieving country.

A Saudi-Iranian Rapprochement Is Harmful to American Interests

By Martin Sieff

In spite of the fact that both countries are nominally Islamic republics, Saudi Arabia and Iran have long been at odds over several issues. Among these issues is religion; the Saudi Arabian population is composed of mostly Sunni Muslims, while the majority of Iranians are Shiite Muslims. Another is the conflict between the Palestinians and the Israelis. Historically, Saudi Arabia supported the Palestinians but was amenable to Western efforts to reach a peace settlement. On the other hand, Iran actively supported Islamic Shiite groups throughout the 1980s and early 1990s that assaulted Israeli military posts and civilian settlements in the West Bank and Gaza Strip. However, Saudi and Iranian positions on the Palestinian-Israeli conflict gradually converged in the second half of the 1990s and the early part of the twenty-first century. Martin Sieff, a senior news analyst for United Press International, argues that the rapprochement between Saudi Arabia and Iran is a result of a shift in power within the Saudi government, changes in the international oil market, and the start of the second Palestinian intifada in September 2001. Sieff concludes that closer ties between Saudi Arabia and Iran will likely cause significant problems for the United States and Israel in the future.

S audi Arabia and Iran are regional rivals whose traditional approach to the Israel-Palestinian conflict has been diametrically opposite. But now they are moving closer together on that and other

Martin Sieff, "The Saudi-Iranian Alliance: United by Oil," www.nationalreview.com, April 26, 2002. Copyright © 2002 by National Review, Inc., 215 Lexington Ave., New York, NY 10016. Reproduced by permission.

issues, with probable immense consequences for the United States and the entire world.

Over the past 20 years, Saudi Arabia has been moderate on both global oil prices and in its approach to the Israel-Arab conflict. The Saudis strongly support the Palestinians. But until recently, that support has been low-key. And the Saudis, quietly, strongly supported the Oslo Peace Process over the past decade from its initiation in August-September 1993 to its breakdown after the July 2000 Camp David II summit.

However, these relatively moderate policies have become increasingly hard-line over the past three years because of the replacement of the pro-American King Fahd by the tougher Crown Prince Abdullah bin Abdul Aziz and because of the collapse of the Oslo Process and start of the second Palestinian intifada. Now Saudi and Iranian policies on the Israel-Arab conflict are converging—although the domestic reasons for this are very different in each country.

The Convergence of Saudi and Iranian Foreign Policies

In Saudi Arabia, supporting the Palestinians is seen as a lightning rod to distract a population feared to be far more radical than its rulers. In Iran, supporting the Palestinians serves the same purpose. But there the aim is to distract a population that is believed to be far less radical and hard-line than its leaders.

The Bush administration has consistently wooed Saudi Arabia and turned a blind eye to the two-faced nature of many of its policies. At the same time, it has repeatedly ignored and failed to woo more moderate elements in Iran.

President Bush's now famous—and notorious—inclusion of Iran in an international "axis of evil" in his State of the Union speech in February 2002 is widely regarded in Tehran and, indeed, throughout the region, as a crucial turning point. Since then, pro-American sentiments in Tehran have been less enthusiastically expressed and popular feeling has coalesced anew behind a government that, for all its faults, is seen as a representative of the national interest against a potential direct threat from the dominant superpower.

Iran in contrast to Saudi Arabia has always been a hard-line hawk on the Israel-Arab conflict. All through the years of the Oslo Peace Process, its support for the Islamic Shiite fundamentalist Hezbollah, or Party of God, guerrilla group in southern Lebanon never wavered.

Iran has also always been a hawk on setting global oil prices. That is because the Iranians know they do not have the luxury of time to

take the long-term view. Their oil reserves are running out and they
have to maximize revenues from them as fast as they can. To para-
phrase John Maynard Keynes, in the long term, they may not be dead
but they will be paupers.

Throughout the 1980s and 90s, the Saudis could afford to take a
long-term view of the oil market and allow prices to remain relatively low. They did not want to kill the Reagan and Clinton-era economic booms in the United States as these were the driving forces
in global economic growth and soaring demand for their product.
Therefore during those two decades, Saudi energy and Israel-
Palestinian conflict policies were both generally supportive of U.S.
interests and initiatives.

A Dramatic Change in Saudi Policy

In the past few years, however, that has been changing dramatically
for a variety of reasons. First, the ailing King Fahd, effective ruler of
the Desert Kingdom for nearly a quarter of a century as crown prince
under King Khaled and then as monarch in his own right finally had
to relinquish the reins of power because of his failing health. His half-
brother, Crown Prince Abdullah, took over and has cautiously but
steadily followed a policy of strengthening ties to powerful, potentially hostile neighbors like Iraq and Iran while distancing himself
from the United States.

Second, in 1999, Crown Prince Abdullah negotiated a radical and
ambitious production cutting agreement with Iran to shore up global
oil prices. U.S. policymakers and market analysts scoffed. The Organization of Petroleum Exporting Countries was a dead duck, they
said. Its old market stranglehold of the 1970s had been rendered ob-
solete by two decades of new oil fields coming on line around the
world and radically more advanced technology becoming easily
available to access them.

Nevertheless, Crown Prince Abdullah's "old-fashioned" and "out-
of-date" deal with the Iranians worked. Global oil prices soared by
350 percent in less than two years, though they then fell significantly.
But now they are showing signs of rising again.

Third, Crown Prince Abdullah's succession to effective power in
Riyadh was followed by the collapse of the Oslo Peace Process in
the Camp David Summit and the start of the second, or "al Aksa,"
Palestinian intifada at the end of September 2001.

Since then, radical pro-Palestinian sentiment throughout the Middle East including Saudi Arabia itself has remorselessly intensified.
And under Abdullah's quiet-but-firm direction, Saudi policy and tacit
encouragement for tougher policies and public statements has inten-

sified too. The recent Saudi telethon to raise millions of dollars for the families of Palestinian suicide bombers was a dramatic but entirely consistent example of this process. So was Riyadh's striking failure to even pretend to take disciplinary action against the Saudi ambassador to Britain when he published a poem celebrating the slaughter of Israeli civilians, including women and children, by suicide bombers.

The Consequences of Saudi-Iranian Convergence

The Bush administration has shown itself repeatedly willfully blind to the radical changes taking place in Saudi policy under Crown Prince Abdullah's direction and they have also shown themselves deaf and blind to the prospects of improving relations with Iran offered by President Mohamed Khatami in Tehran. As a result Saudi policies are changing in ways inimical to U.S. interests while Iranian polices are not changing at all.

The global oil crisis of the 1970s was only possible because Saudi Arabia and Iran, the two greatest oil producers in the world, teamed up to enforce their mutual colossal energy clout. The 1979 Iranian Revolution had the paradoxical effect of ensuring 20 years of global economic growth based on cheap oil supplies because the new Iranian rulers were so hostile to the Saudis. But now, for the first time in almost a quarter of a century, Saudi and Iranian policies are converging again.

This is good news for the Palestinians and bad news for the Israelis. It may also prove to be very bad news for the United States and the Bush administration.

A Saudi Plan for Peace Between Israel and the Palestinians

By Abdullah Ibn Abdul Aziz Al Saud

Crown Prince Abdullah Ibn Abdul Aziz Al Saud was born in 1924 in Riyadh, Saudi Arabia—one of many sons born to the founder of the Saudi state, Abdul Aziz Al Saud. In 1962, Abdullah was appointed commander of the Saudi Arabian National Guard by his uncle, King Faisal, and was later named First Deputy Prime Minister and Crown Prince in 1982 after his brother, King Fahd, ascended the Saudi throne. After his brother suffered a stroke in 1995, Abdullah took over the daily management of the Saudi state, effectively becoming the highest ranking official in the Saudi government. In the passage that follows, Abdullah presents a plan for peace between Israel and the Palestinians that he formally unveiled at the Arab League summit in Beirut, Lebanon, on March 27, 2002. The plan offers Israel full diplomatic relations with the member states of the Arab League in exchange for the withdrawal of Israeli troops from Palestinian territory in the West Bank and Gaza Strip, areas that Israel has occupied since the end of the six-day war of 1967. Abdullah's proposal represented a significant shift in Saudi Arabia's relations with Israel and the Palestinians, as it is one of the few times in recent history that its political leaders chose to become actively involved in the peace process rather than deferring to American initiatives.

I n spite of all that has happened—and what still may happen—the primary issue in the heart and mind of every person in our Arab and Islamic nation is the restoration of legitimate rights in Palestine, Syria and Lebanon.

Abdullah Ibn Abdul Aziz Al Saud, speech before the Arab League's Annual Summit, Beirut, Lebanon, March 27, 2002.

These rights, which are bound to the cherished occupied lands, can not be erased from memory, nor will the passage of time diminish their importance. No right is lost that has an advocate behind it. Those who follow the intifada of our brothers in Palestine, which has the support of all Arabs and Muslims, realise that steadfastness will not wither, that bravery will not retreat, and that justice will prevail.

Every person in Palestine—young and old—understands that the way to the liberation of his land and soil is either through steadfastness and struggle, or a just and comprehensive peace. It is therefore incumbent on the Israeli government to realise and understand this and deal with it by embarking on a new path, and that is the path of peace.

My dear brethren: the noble people of the Arab and Islamic nation: when the Arabs opted for peace as a strategic choice, they did not do so out of crippling desperation or debilitating weakness, and Israel is mistaken if it believes that it can impose an unjust peace by force.

We embarked upon the peace process with open eyes and clear minds, and we have not accepted then, nor will we accept now, that this process is transformed into a non-binding obligation imposed by one party on the other. Peace is a free and voluntary choice made by two equal parties, and it can not survive if it is based on oppression and humiliation.

Land for Peace

The peace process is based on a clear principle: land for peace. This principle is accepted by the international community as a whole, and is embodied in U.N. Security Council resolutions 242 and 338, and was adopted by the Madrid conference in 1991. It was confirmed by the resolutions of the European Community and other regional organisations, and re-emphasised once more this month, by U.N. Security Council resolution 1397.

My esteemed brethren: it is clear in our minds, and in the minds of our brethren in Palestine, Syria and Lebanon, that the only acceptable objective of the peace process is the full Israeli withdrawal from all the occupied Arab territories, the establishment of an independent Palestinian state with al-Quds al-Shareef (East Jerusalem) as its capital, and the return of refugees.

Without moving towards this objective, the peace process is an exercise in futility and a play on words and a squandering of time which perpetuates the cycle of violence. The return to the negotiating table is a meaningless endeavour if the negotiations do not produce tangible and positive results, as has been the case for the past 10 years.

Allow me at this point to directly address the Israeli people, to say to them that the use of violence, for more than 50 years, has only resulted in more violence and destruction, and that the Israeli people are as far as they have ever been from security and peace, notwithstanding military superiority and despite efforts to subdue and oppress.

Peace emanates from the heart and mind, and not from the barrel of a cannon, or the exploding warhead of a missile. The time has come for Israel to put its trust in peace after it has gambled on war for decades without success. Israel, and the world, must understand that peace and the retention of the occupied Arab territories are incompatible and impossible to reconcile or achieve.

I would further say to the Israeli people that if their government abandons the policy of force and oppression and embraces true peace, we will not hesitate to accept the right of the Israeli people to live in security with the people of the region.

We believe in fighting in self-defence and to deter aggression. But we also believe in peace when it is based on justice and equity, and when it brings an end to conflict. Only within the context of true peace can normal relations flourish between the people of the region and allow the region to pursue development rather than war and destruction.

Dear brethren, in light of the above, and in this place with you and amongst you, and with your backing and that of the Almighty, I propose that the Arab summit put forward a clear and unanimous initiative addressed to the United Nations Security Council based on two basic issues: normal relations and security for Israel in exchange for full withdrawal from all occupied Arab territories, recognition of an independent Palestinian state with al-Quds al-Shareef (East Jerusalem) as its capital, and the return of refugees. At the same time, I appeal to all friendly countries throughout the world to support this noble humanitarian proposal which seeks to remove the danger of destructive wars and the establishment of peace for all the inhabitants of the region, without exception.

I ask God Almighty to guide us to the correct decision, and to provide us with the determination of the believer, for he is our Lord and ultimate benefactor. God's peace and blessing be upon you.

The West Should Dismantle the Al Saud Monarchy

By Mark Steyn

Mark Steyn is a columnist for the National Post *in Canada and a regular contributor to the* Spectator *in the United Kingdom. He has also been a long-time theater critic for the* New Criterion. *In the following selection, Steyn argues that Saudi Arabia is not only an unreliable ally to Western countries, but that it is responsible, either directly or indirectly, for the September 11, 2001, attacks against New York and Washington, D.C. Steyn states his concern about the Saudi educational system, which in some cases advocates a violent interpretation of Islam, as well as Saudi Arabia's tendency to support radical Islamic groups in other regions of the world. According to Steyn, the best remedy for Islamic fundamentalism and the growth of terrorist activity in the Middle East is for the United States and its allies to depose the Saudi monarchy and divide Saudi territory among the remaining kingdoms in the Persian Gulf.*

Joanne Jacobs, formerly a columnist with the *San Jose Mercury News*, spotted a dandy headline in her old paper in March 2002. A Muslim mob, you'll recall, had attacked a train full of Hindus, an unfortunate development which the *Mercury News* reported to its readers thus: 'Religious Tensions Kill 57 In India'.

Ah, those religious tensions'll kill you every time. Is there a Preparation H for religious tension? Or an extra-strength Tylenol, in case you feel a sudden attack coming on? I haven't looked at the *San Jose Mercury News* for 12 September 2001, but I'm assuming the front page read, 'Religious Tensions Kill 3,000 In New York', a particularly bad outbreak.

Mark Steyn, "Down with Saudi Arabia: Mark Steyn Says That It Is Time to Destroy the Arab Kingdom Which, Directly or Indirectly, Is Responsible for 11 September," *The Spectator*, vol. 288, March 9, 2002, pp. 18–19. Copyright © 2002 by The Spectator, Ltd. Reproduced by permission.

If I were an Islamic fundamentalist, I'd be wondering what I had to do to get bad press. The *New York Times* had a picture recently of a party of Palestinian suicide bombers looking like Klansmen, all dressed up and ready to blow. They were captioned 'Hamas activists'. Take my advice and try not to be standing anywhere near an activist when he activates himself. You gotta hand it to the Islamofascists: while the usual doom-mongers are now querying whether America's up to fighting a war on two fronts (Afghanistan and Iraq), the Islamabaddies blithely open up new fronts every couple of weeks. At the World Trade Center, Muslim terrorists killed mainly Christians. In Israel, they're killing mainly Jews. In India, they're killing mainly Hindus. Let's not get into the Sudan or the Philippines. Now, OK, there are two sides to every dispute, but these days one side can pretty well be predicted: Muslims v. Jews, Muslims v. Christians, Muslims v. Hindus, Muslims v. [Your Religion Here]. If war were tennis, they'd be Grand Slam champions: they'll play on anything—lawn, clay, rubble. And yet the more they kill, the more frantically the press cranks out the 'Islam is a religion of peace' editorials.

Saudi Arabia Is Not a Reliable Ally

Now it would be absurd to claim that all Muslims are terrorists. But the idea that the forces at play in New York, Palestine, Tora Bora and Kashmir are some sort of tiny unrepresentative extremist fringe of Islam is equally ludicrous. Recently, the *Boston Globe* reported from the Saudi town of Abha on the subtleties of the kingdom's education system: 'At a public high school in this provincial town in the southwest part of the country, 10th-grade classes are forced to memorise from a Ministry of Education textbook entitled "Monotheism" that is replete with anti-Christian and anti-Jewish bigotry and violent interpretations of Islamic scripture. A passage on page 64 under the title "Judgment Day" says, "The Hour will not come until Muslims will fight the Jews, and Muslims will kill all the Jews."'

That's pretty straightforward, isn't it? In fact, pretty much everything about Saudi Arabia, except for the urbane evasions of their Washington ambassador, Prince Bandar, is admirably straightforward. Saudi citizens were, for the most part, responsible for 11 September. The Saudi government funds the madrassahs in Pakistan which are doing their best to breed a South Asian branch office of Saudi Wahhabism. Admittedly, the Saudis are less directly responsible for the Israeli-Palestinian conflict, except insofar as they have a vested interest in it as a distraction from other matters. So, if we don't want to be beastly about Muslims in general, we could at least be beastly about the House of Saud in particular.

Instead, the Saudi question has become the ne plus ultra of the Islamo-euphemist approach, and a beloved staple of comment pages and cable news shows. By now, 'The Saudis Are Our Friends' may even have its own category in the Pulitzers. Usually this piece turns up after the Saudis have done something not terribly friendly—refused to let Washington use the US bases in Saudi Arabia, or even to meet with Tony Blair. Then the apparently vast phalanx of former US ambassadors to Saudi Arabia fans out across the *New York Times*, CNN, Nightline, etc., to insist that, au contraire, the Saudis have been 'enormously helpful.' At what? Recommending a decent restaurant in Mayfair?

The Saudi Plan for Peace in the Middle East

Charles Freeman, a former ambassador to the kingdom and now president of something called the Middle East Policy Council, offered a fine example of the genre when he revealed that Crown Prince Abdullah, the head honcho since King Fahd had his stroke, was 'personally anguished' by developments in the Middle East and that that was why he had proposed his 'peace plan'. If, indeed, he has proposed it—to anyone other than Thomas Friedman of the *New York Times*, that is. And, come to think of it, it was Friedman who proposed it to the Prince—Israel withdraws to the 4 June 1967 lines, Palestinian state, full normalised relations with the Arab League, etc. 'After I laid out this idea,' wrote Friedman, 'the Crown Prince looked at me with mock astonishment and said, "Have you broken into my desk?"

"'No," I said, wondering what he was talking about.

"'The reason I ask is that this is exactly the idea I had in mind. . . .'"

What a coincidence! Apparently, the Prince had 'drafted a speech along those lines' and 'it is in my desk'. It's just that he hadn't got around to delivering the speech. Seems an awful waste of a good speech. Unless—perish the thought—it's just something he keeps in his desk to flatter visiting American correspondents. In any case, it's the same peace plan the Saudis dust off every ten years—they proposed it in 1991, and before that in 1981. It's just a couple of months late this time round. But book a meeting around October 2011 with King Abdullah (as he plans on being by then) and he'll gladly propose it to you one mo' time. Prince Abdullah has no interest in Palestinians: it's easier for a Palestinian to emigrate to Tipton and become a subject of the Queen of England than to emigrate to Riyadh and become a subject of King Fahd. But the Prince's peace plan usefully changes the subject from more embarrassing matters—such as the kingdom's role in the events of 11 September.

Saudi Arabia's Role in the September 11 Attacks

There are only two convincing positions on the House of Saud and what happened that grim day: a) They're indirectly responsible for it; b) They're directly responsible for it. There's a lot of evidence for the former—the Saudi funding of the madrassahs, etc.—and a certain amount of not yet totally compelling evidence for the latter—a Saudi 'humanitarian aid' office in the Balkans set up by a member of the royal family which appears to be a front for terrorism. Reasonable people can disagree on whether it's (a) or (b) but for Americans to argue that the Saudis are our allies in the war on terrorism is like Ron Goldman's dad joining O.J. in his search for the real killers. The advantage of this thesis to fellows like Charles Freeman is that it places a premium on their nuance-interpretation skills. Because everything the kingdom does seems to be self-evidently inimical to the West, any old four-year-old can point out that the King is in the altogether hostile mode. It takes an old Saudi hand like Mr. Freeman to draw attention to the subtler shades of meaning, to explain the ancient ways of Araby, by which, say, an adamant refusal to arrest associates of the 11 September hijackers is, in fact, a clear sign of the Saudis' remarkable support for Washington. If the Saudis nuked Delaware, the massed ranks of former ambassadors would be telling Larry King that, obviously, even the best allies have their difficulties from time to time, but this is essentially a little hiccup that can be smoothed over by closer consultation.

Do they know what they're talking about? You'll remember the old-school Kremlinologists, who'd watch the Red Army parades and tip as the coming man the 87-year-old corpse with the luxuriant monobrow and the waxy complexion propped up against the 93-year-old commissar of the Sverdlovsk gasworks and people's hall of culture. The Kremlinologists got everything wrong, of course, and they had only a couple of dozen guys to divine the intentions of. Saudi Arabia has 7,000 princes—at the time of writing; it may be up to 7,600 if you're reading this after lunch. Many of us have never met a Saudi who isn't a prince. Chances are you can find princes to represent any view you want. But the awkward fact is that the dominant faction in the House of Saud right now is anti-American.

Instead of presenting Prince Abdullah with Israeli-Palestinian peace proposals, Americans ought to be handing him US-Saudi peace proposals: clean up your own education system and stop destabilising Asian Muslim culture, for starters. Washington (and London, too) needs to figure out what it wants from Saudi Arabia and whether it's likely to get it from King Fahd and his bloated clan. We already know one thing we're not going to get: the Taleban had two major allies before 11 September, Pakistan and Saudi Arabia, and it's clear the royal house has no inclination to do a Musharraf. If the West has a medium-term aim in the Middle East, it ought to be the evolution of Arabic Islam into something closer to the more moderate Muslim temperament of Turkey or Bangladesh. I know, I know, all these things are relative, but even that modest goal is unattainable under the House of Saud. The royal family derives such legitimacy as it has from its role as the guardian and promoter of Wahhabism. It is, therefore, the ideological font of militant Islamism in the way that Saddam and Boy Assad and Mubarak and the other Arab thugs aren't. Saddam is as Islamic as the wind is blowing: say what you like about the old mass murderer, but his malign activities are not, in that sense, defined by his religion. One cannot say the same for the House of Saud. If the issue is 'religious tensions', who's fomenting them, from Pakistan to the Balkans to America itself? Saudi Arabia should be a 'root cause' we can all agree on.

Removing the Al Saud from Power

But sadly not. John O'Sullivan, former editor of *National Review*, wrote recently that 'reforming the House of Saud will be a formidable and subtle task. But it offers a great deal more hope for everyone than blithely burning it down.' I disagree. Reforming the House of Saud is all but impossible. Lavish economic engagement with the West has only entrenched it more firmly in its barbarism. 'Stability' means letting layabout princes use Western oil revenues to seduce their people into anti-Western nihilism. On the other hand, blithely burning it down offers quite a bit of hope, given that no likely replacement would provide the ideological succour to the Islamakazis that Saud-endorsed Wahhabism does. My own view—maps available on request—is that the Muslim holy sites and most of the interior should go to the Hashemites of Jordan, and what's left should be divided between the less wacky Gulf emirs. That should be the policy goal, even if for the moment it's pursued covertly rather than by daisy cutters.

Borders are not sacrosanct. The House of Saud is not royal; they are merely nomads who found a sugar daddy. There's no good reason why every time a soccer mom fills her Chevy Suburban she should be helping fund some toxic madrassah. In this instance, destabilisation is our friend.

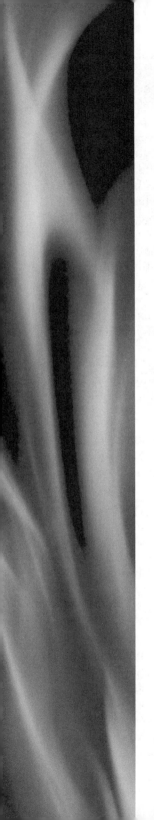

 **CHAPTER 4**

The Prospects for Reform in Saudi Arabia

Saudi Economic and Social Reform Will Come Slowly

By Eric Rouleau

Eric Rouleau was the French ambassador to Tunisia from 1985 to 1986 and to Turkey from 1988 to 1992. He is currently an independent writer with articles published in several international affairs magazines, including Foreign Affairs. *Rouleau examines the domestic social and economic conditions in Saudi Arabia in the excerpt below. According to Rouleau, any change in Saudi Arabia, which suffers from chronic underdevelopment in its economy and educational system, must come slowly to avoid infighting in the royal family and the total collapse of the Al Saud dynasty.*

Saudi Arabia faces a serious domestic crisis that could destabilize the regime in the long run. "We live in a schizophrenic state," one prominent member of the royal family recently remarked. The expression, heard frequently in upper-class Saudi homes, is by no means an exaggeration. The foreign visitor arriving in Riyadh is immediately struck by the kingdom's modernity; by one of the most spacious airports in the world, luxurious and functional; by the wide, tree-lined boulevards of the capital, with elegant buildings, proud towers, American-style shopping centers, and cyber-cafés; and by the kingdom's computerized administration and businesses.

But there exists another Saudi Arabia, equally striking. This is the country that, since the demise of the Taliban, now bears the dubious distinction of being the most rigorous theocracy in the Islamic world. . . . In this Saudi Arabia, the Koran serves as the constitution and is interpreted as prohibiting such things as movie houses, theaters, discotheques, and concerts. Fully half of the population—namely, Saudi

Eric Rouleau, "Trouble in the Kingdom," *Foreign Affairs*, vol. 81, July/August 2002, pp. 75–89.

women—are banned from public spaces unless they cloak themselves in black from head to toe. Women are also treated as legal minors: instead of having her own individual identity card or passport, for example, a Saudi woman is listed on the documents of her male guardian (although starting in 2002, women can now obtain their own cards, but only at their guardians' request and with their guarantee). A Saudi woman cannot undertake the most routine administrative procedure, open a bank account, purchase property, work, or travel without the express approval of her guardian. Nor are women in Saudi Arabia allowed to drive. Officially, they can work only in two fields: education and medicine, and even there they must be segregated from their male colleagues. As a result of such strictures, tens of thousands of female university graduates do not work outside their homes. The mingling of the sexes is likewise forbidden in schools; universities require male professors teaching women's classes to give their lectures through a closed-circuit one-way television system, ensuring that the lecturers cannot see their students.

Not only women suffer under this system. At least 65 percent of the Saudi population is now under 25 years of age, and the frustrations felt by these youngsters are enormous. The kingdom's puritanical rules prevent young people from mixing with the opposite sex or enjoying the kinds of pastimes taken for granted elsewhere. Without meaningful outlets for their energy or ways to spend spare time, increasing numbers are turning to the illicit consumption of alcohol and drugs. They are also turning to satellite television and to the Internet, which serve only to broaden their horizons and give them a window on the modern world—making their restrictions all the more onerous and helping ensure that their aspirations differ markedly from those of their elders.

A Failed Educational System

Saudi Arabia's educational system also prevents many young men from finding productive jobs. The Saudi media are good at pointing out that local schools have churned out a mediocre work force ill adapted to the needs of modern corporations. But they fail to mention a salient explanation for this problem: 30 to 40 percent of the course hours in schools are devoted to studying scripture. The teaching of non-Islamic philosophy, meanwhile, is banned. As a result, Saudi university graduates end up more qualified to analyze holy texts than to work as engineers, architects, computer specialists, or managers. And this in turn means that many heads of Saudi companies prefer to employ foreigners rather than locals; in fact, a full two-thirds of the work force is now foreign. Expatriates are considered more competent than Saudis, and cheaper: they can be paid four to five times less than citizens. These factors together contribute to an unemployment rate of about 30 percent among Saudi men and 95 percent for women. These figures, moreover, are constantly rising because of a population growth rate that is among the highest in the world (more than three percent annually, birth control being seen as contrary to Islam), and because of a general failure of job creation. "We are the only country in the world that imports the unemployed from other countries in order to swell the ranks of the unemployed among its own people," quips Askar Enazy [a professor of international relations].

The resulting social tensions have begun to take various forms. Among them has been a significant drop in marriage rates. Unable to afford the traditional dowry, many young Saudi men are now doomed to a prolonged celibacy. At the same time, growing numbers of young women are refusing to marry men chosen for them by their families, men whom their would-be brides are not allowed to meet before their wedding night. As a result, an estimated two-thirds of Saudi women now between 16 and 30 years of age cannot, or will not, marry.

Economic Woes in Saudi Arabia

Aggravating Saudi Arabia's general social malaise are severe economic problems. Business leaders who lack connections to the royal family and the exceptional privileges these bring must struggle in an environment that discourages commerce. Potential lenders and investors are stymied by obstacles such as an archaic judicial system based on the *shari'a* (Islamic law) and applied by religious courts; laws forbidding the establishment of local insurance companies on the grounds that they practice "usury," forbidden by Islam; and the non-transparency of state accounts. Saudi citizens keep much of their money abroad; these foreign investments, mainly in the United States, are estimated by Western bankers to total anywhere from $700 billion to a trillion dollars. Saudis have not brought this money home, not even since the September 11 attacks. But as a result, there is not enough money for local investment, and the kingdom's private sector generates only a third of Gross Domestic Product (GDP).

In the past, the Saudi state was able to use oil money to compensate for the shortcomings of private enterprise. But this is no longer possible; in fact, contrary to widespread perceptions abroad, Saudi Arabia, which should be the richest nation in the Gulf, is now far worse off than many of its neighbors. The Saudi budget has run a deficit ever since the vast outlays of the Gulf War a decade ago. That war cost the kingdom more than $60 billion, mostly to cover the United States' military outlay during the operation. Since then, Riyadh has spent tens of billions of additional dollars, often uselessly, on American weaponry. Thanks to such crushing expenditures, the kingdom now has the highest indebtedness in the Gulf: $171 billion in domestic loans and $35 billion in foreign credits, or 107 percent of the country's GDP. Unstable oil revenues are hardly sufficient to repay this debt or even to compensate state employees (who number more than a million); government salaries have already been frozen for years.

Inevitably, the population overall has become poorer: per capita income plunged from $28,600 in 1981 (equivalent to that of the United States the same year) to $6,800 in 2001. By comparison, the average per capita revenue in Abu Dhabi is $36,000, and in Qatar it is $26,000. To redress the situation, Crown Prince Abdullah has set two general goals: to modernize the state apparatus, and to liberalize the economy. To attract foreign capital, critically important for re-launching productive enterprises, generous incentives are being offered to potential investors. Prince Abdullah has also appointed a particularly enlightened and dynamic man, Prince Abdullah bin Faisal bin Turki, to head the Saudi Arabian General Investment Authority, and the latter prince has managed in one year to increase investments by more than $10 billion. The opening of the gas sector to foreign companies—an unprecedented step since the nationalization of the Arabian American Oil Company (Aramco) in 1976—is also expected to bring in an additional $30 billion by 2012. And a vast privatization program, if ever implemented, should inject still more into the economy. Draft legislation is being prepared to legalize insurance companies, to introduce the right to a defense in the courts, to establish labor regulations, and to create a human rights organization—all positive signs.

The Debate over Domestic Reforms

Not everyone has been impressed by the recent initiatives, however. Prince Talal, for example—another of King Fahd's half brothers, and a man long known as one of the most liberal members of the royal family—has welcomed Abdullah's reforms but argues that they are inadequate to move Saudi Arabia fully into the twenty-first century. "In order to survive," Talal told me, "the kingdom has to adapt itself to the new world and become fully integrated into the globalized economy." To do so, he believes, more fundamental reforms are needed. Saudi Arabia must join the World Trade Organization (WTO), for example; indeed, Riyadh has been trying to do just that for seven years but has been denied entry for its failure to make the required judicial, social, and political changes. This irks the prince. "As a patriot and a democrat," he declared, "I would like to see my country endowed with a transparent political system and with laws that are passed by a representative assembly, which would also approve the state budget." Among other items on the prince's wish list are equal rights for women, a totally independent judiciary, the removal of archaic laws from the books, the holding of municipal elections, a modernized educational system adapted to the needs of the country, the "humanization"of penal sanctions ("some of which were inherited from pre-Islamic times," according to the prince), a liberalization of social life (for example, allowing theaters and movie houses), and "state neutrality and tolerance toward all religions." "Nothing in my proposals is contrary to Islam," argues Talal. "Quite the contrary; the religious and political foundations of the kingdom would be consolidated through them."

The conservative wing of the royal family disagrees, however, maintaining that the reforms would destabilize the regime by provoking the opposition of both the religious establishment and a conservative population imbued with Wahhabi dogma. The reformists counter that there is nothing so revolutionary about the proposals; they point out that during the reign of Ibn Saud, the founder of the kingdom, churches were allowed to function, banks collected and paid interest, and women legally enjoyed more freedom than they do today. Reformers also point out that Ibn Saud and one of his successors, King Faisal, managed to impose unpopular reforms—sometimes through the use of force—including the suppression of slavery, the opening of schools for girls, and the introduction of television. And they did all this without undermining the regime. Moreover, although reformers recognize that the kingdom was built on an alliance between the Wahhabi clergy and the House of Saud, they note that the government was always meant to maintain the upper hand, in keeping with an Islamic tradition that recognizes the primacy of the temporal over the spiritual in state affairs.

Factors Leading to the Dominance of the Clergy

In any alliance, however, it is the balance of power that determines which partner dominates. From the 1940s to the 1970s, the House of Saud held all the cards and thus overshadowed the clergy. Two factors have since helped change that situation. First, the royal family has lost influence due to the excesses certain of its members, who have been accused of abusing their excessive privileges, of leading dissolute lives marked by corruption and wasteful spending, and of inordinate submissiveness to U.S. wishes. A second factor has been the emergence of a militant fringe of Islamists under the tutelage of the Muslim Brotherhood. These radicals, such as Osama bin Laden, have called into question the very legitimacy of the al Saud dynasty, and although it is impossible to gauge the precise impact of such propaganda, it appears to have resonated. Meanwhile, the ongoing deterioration of economic and social conditions has reduced the clout of the ruling family still further.

When first faced with these challenges, the Saudi royals made an ill-conceived decision to come to terms with their adversaries rather than confront them. When an armed revolt by Islamic extremists broke out in 1979 in Mecca, the authorities dealt ruthlessly with the perpetrators but were strangely indulgent toward those who had inspired them. A similar situation followed the Gulf War of 1991. The war was opposed by a number of religious figures, some of whom were jailed, but those given long prison terms were eventually released early, and political concessions were made to the radical wing of the clergy. Religious education was intensified in the schools and universities, including in science departments; girls' schools were placed under the direct control of the religious authorities (although the ministry of education reportedly regained jurisdiction in spring 2002), women were forbidden to sing on radio or television or in public; and increased powers were granted to the *mutawaun* (volunteers), a clerical police force whose task is to "promote virtue" by making sure that public establishments close during the hours of prayer (five times a day) and by taking into custody women and young people whose conduct is not in keeping with "Islamic morals." The clergy was also given effective censorship power over the media, especially radio and television.

These concessions, according to numerous reformists, were as unnecessary as they were dangerous. They were made to a vocal minority that should have been suppressed rather than placated. Reformists argue that the great majority of the religious establishment—officials whose salaries are paid by the state—would have remained loyal to the royal family without the compromises. The fidelity of this silent majority of clergy has long been virtually guaranteed by the many privileges they enjoy, privileges that enable them to enrich themselves through speculative ventures—for example, by selling at high prices land received as a gift from the state. Afforded the same diplomatic immunity as members of the royal family, clerics cannot be arrested or put on trial without the explicit authorization of the palace. Small wonder, then, that most remain loyal to their benefactors. Indeed, this loyalty was recently demonstrated by their quiet acquiescence to Prince Abdullah's [Palestinian-Israeli] peace plan.

And yet the state has consistently bowed to militants and conservatives, and liberals—religious and otherwise—have been condemned to silence. The authorities even intervened in August 2001 to censor a Web site that the reformists had established in London with secret financing by certain members of the royal family. Moreover, conservative clerics have been allowed to dominate the media. As a result, there has been no national debate on the gradual transformation of the kingdom, and reformers have found few outlets to garner support.

Contrary to the contention of the conservatives, however, most Saudis would be amenable to the modernization of their state—if it could be carried out without violating the fundamental principles of Islam, as has been achieved in some moderate Muslim countries. Especially supportive of such reforms are Saudi women, young people, business leaders, technocrats, and the enlightened intelligentsia—not to mention the liberal wing of the royal family. Together, these forces make up more than half of the population. They believe that change need not be destabilizing; according to one young prince with an important government position, "democratization would have the advantage of increasing the legitimacy of the ruling family. Unfortunately," he continued, "we are ruled by a gerontocracy that prefers the artificial comfort of the status quo."

Reform Will Only Come Slowly

As for which side will prevail, Enazy, for his part, is pessimistic. He believes that the Wahhabi kingdom is going through "a Brezhnevian period. But no one here wants to play the role of [Mikhail] Gorbachev, who ushered in the collapse of the communist system." Rather than Russia, however, the more apposite analogy may be with Iran. Crown Prince Abdullah, like Iranian President Muhammad Khatami, has become the standard-bearer for a reformist majority that lacks the means to realize its aspirations. Both leaders are prisoners of a political and religious system dominated by a conservative faction that, although perhaps not representative of the populace, nonetheless controls the levers of power. Prince Abdullah cannot act without a consensus within the royal family, which is dominated by a powerful group of his half brothers known as the "Sudeiri Seven." This group includes the king and his six full brothers (whose mother belongs to the Sudeiri family); they control key positions in the realm, including the defense ministry, the interior ministry, the treasury, and the governorships of the main provinces. Although the royal family is far from monolithic, none of its more liberal members is prepared to confront this powerful bloc; after all, dissension within the House of Saud could unleash dangerous chaos.

Having said that, the reformists have failed to capitalize on what strengths they do possess. Unorganized and amorphous, they represent various schools of thought and segments of society, from business leaders calling for transparency in state affairs to democrats advocating universal suffrage, from constitutional monarchists and Wahhabi modernists to determined secularists. Given this lack of cohesion, even liberal members of the royal family fear that, if given free rein, the reformists, lacking any one clear agenda, could get out of hand.

The fundamental truth, however, remains that radical change would spell the end of the al Saud family's absolute power and the privileges enjoyed by some 3,000 princes and the hundreds of families linked to them. This is the real source of the government's conservatism, and helps explain why Prince Abdullah, like President Khatami—both of whom have a stake in the survival of the system—has proceeded so cautiously. There is no doubt that the crown prince fully intends to carry on with his efforts to modernize the state and to promote economic development. But the extent and the pace of his reforms will depend less on his intentions than on the internal tensions of a society riddled with contradictions, and on the external pressures engendered by the irresistible push toward globalization.

The Al Saud Dynasty Will Remain in Power

By Bill Powell

After the terrorist attacks on New York and Washington, D.C., in September 2001, many foreign policy analysts turned their attention to Saudi Arabia, which was the nation of origin for fifteen of the nineteen individuals responsible for the attacks. According to many of these analysts, the fundamentalist political culture that produced the fifteen hijackers would eventually produce a backlash against a corrupt and oppressive regime in Saudi Arabia. In the following excerpt, Bill Powell, who is a former foreign correspondent at Newsweek *magazine and is currently the Beijing Bureau Chief for* Fortune *magazine, argues that the prophecies of doom for the Saudi monarchy were greatly exaggerated. Instead, Powell states that the Saudi economic and political systems are designed in a way that insulates the Al Saud family from any attempt by Saudi dissidents to remove them from power.*

Of the countries "in play" since Sept. 11—those whose futures matter more to the rest of the world than any others—two stand out. One is Pakistan, which has nuclear arms and formerly sponsored the Taliban regime. Pakistan is also home to its own virulently fundamentalist movement—people and political parties who seek the imposition of an Islamic state—and those ranks will no doubt soon be joined by thousands of routed Taliban fighters fleeing Afghanistan. They will not be well disposed to President Pervez Musharraf, who sold them out to join the U.S. coalition in the pursuit of bin Laden. Instability in Pakistan, and the possibility of the "Islamic bomb" falling into the hands of angry *jihadi*, is the stuff of genuine nightmares.

The second country of consequence is Saudi Arabia. And the rea-

Bill Powell, "Is Saudi Arabia Headed for a Fall?" *Fortune*, vol. 144, December 10, 2001, pp. 193–200. Copyright © 2001 by *Fortune*. Reproduced by permission.

son for that, as everyone knows, is oil. Saudi oil is why the U.S. fought the Gulf war. It's why the U.S. still has some 5,000 troops stewing in the desert south of Riyadh. It's why 19 of their brothers and sisters were blown up in 1996, when terrorists attacked the al Khobar barracks.

The Saudis have more than 25% of the world's proven reserves. They are the biggest producer and the biggest exporter, and though the U.S. buys more oil from Canada these days, we are the Saudis' biggest export market. They need us, and we need them. It is a marriage rooted in nothing more than the geological accident that, millennia ago, put more hydrocarbons under this desert than in any other place in the world.

You can curse your luck and rail at the gods, or you can deal with reality. And ever since Franklin Delano Roosevelt gave Abdul Aziz, King Fahd's father, his word that America was a friend (and defender) of the kingdom, the U.S. has dealt with reality. Through thick and thin it has cultivated the kingdom's rulers as "moderate" allies in the Arab world: from the Nasser era of pan-Arab nationalism to the Six-Day War in 1967 to the Iranian revolution [in 1979] to the liberation of Kuwait [in 1991]. And through it all, as Prince Turki al Faisal, the former head of the General Intelligence Department (GID) the Saudis' version of the CIA, said in an interview, "we proudly flaunted our friendship with the United States."

Saudi-American Relations After Sept. 11

But nothing has tested the relationship between these two countries the way Sept. 11 has. It is not simply that bin Laden is a Saudi, or that 15 of the 19 hijackers who attacked the U.S. were Saudis, or that, prior to 1998 at least, the Saudis had deep ties to the Taliban regime that harbored bin Laden and the rest of al Qaeda's high command. Since Sept. 11 has come a wave of stories in the establishment press in the U.S. that have portrayed Saudi Arabia in a brutally unflattering light. It was accused of not cooperating fully with the pursuit of bin Laden's financial network; of impeding the investigation into the hijackers; of not allowing the U.S. use of the highly sophisticated Prince Sultan air base (built by the U.S.) as a key command-and-control center in the war in Afghanistan.

Then came reams of copy about Saudi financing of Islamic schools in Pakistan, called *madrasahs*, whose students, as Jessica Stern, a former staffer on Bill Clinton's National Security Council, puts it, become "canon fodder for the *jihadi*"—the Islamic warriors who will carry on bin Laden's anti-American campaign even if, by the time you read this, his corpse has been dragged out of a bombed cave in southern Afghanistan. As if that weren't bad enough, the Saudis' own educational system, the stories pointed out, is increasingly dominated by Islamic schools and universities, with textbooks that contain passages like this: "It is compulsory for the Muslims to be loyal to each other and to consider the infidels their enemy." Reading this, who in the U.S. would not be thinking, "With friends like these . . ."?

Combine all this with two undeniable facts—that the Saudi economy has serious problems and that there is a level of discontent among the Saudi populace about, among other things, chronic corruption by the royal family—and you get otherwise intelligent people like economist Paul Krugman concluding in the *New York Times* that "everyone now realizes" Saudi Arabia is "another Afghanistan" waiting to happen.

Time out. Everyone take a deep breath. Afghanistan? The analogy more commonly used is Iran in the 1970s—a corrupt, repressive, oil-rich dictatorship central to U.S. security concerns in the Middle East is overthrown by radical fundamentalists. But even that, as we'll see, appears to be a deeply flawed comparison.

To be sure, a two-week swing through any country, particularly one as paranoid and secretive as Saudi Arabia, cannot answer all questions. But it can answer some. Start fast with some of the fleeting, post-Sept. 11 accusations about a lack of cooperation in the investigation and the alleged reluctance to let the U.S. use the air base that it built. A senior Saudi official, who did not want to be identified, says that in the wake of the attack, "hundreds" of Saudis in the kingdom have been detained for questioning. Similarly, all the assets associated with Saudi nationals or charities suspected of helping to fund bin Laden, this source told me, were frozen, and to date no one from the U.S. Treasury has been in Riyadh to pursue the matter further. And as for the alleged nonuse of the air base, "on the day that story appeared in your press, 220 uniformed servicemen of the United States military were at the Prince Sultan air base." In informal conversations with several Western diplomats, no one disputed any of this.

All of which is not of great consequence. The fact is, if the Saudis had been the reluctant partners they have been accused of being, the U.S. would have grumbled about it but then gotten back to business. What really matters is the kingdom's long-term stability, and here the issues of fundamentalist religion and economics are central. To say that Saudi Arabia is unlikely to be the next Iran, let alone Afghanistan, is not to say that the House of Saud doesn't preside over a country with serious, and deepening, problems. It does. . . .

Religion and Politics in Saudi Arabia

The House of Saud and the Sunni sect known as Wahhabi are joined at the hip and have been for nearly three centuries. In 1744, the followers of a fierce cleric named Mohammed bin Abdul Wahhab allied with the al Sauds, and together they conquered the territory that today makes up central Saudi Arabia. For most of the years since, the descendants of both clans have ruled the kingdom.

No one in Saudi Arabia denies that the Wahhabi clerics play a critical role in their society. What I learned very quickly during my stay in the country, however, is that the characterization of Wahhabism as a "radical" force and, as such, a source of instability both at home and abroad positively drives the Saudis to distraction. Sitting at his desk in the splashy new King Faisal office complex in Riyadh (built by the construction company owned by the bin Laden family of Jiddah), Prince Turki al Faisal, the ex-spymaster, flashes a hint of anger only once, and it's when I raise this subject. "It is," he snaps, "pure hogwash."

It was going to take a lot longer than two weeks for me to figure out how the Saudis square their vision of Wahhabism—a "quieting, moderating force," as one Saudi businessman told me—with the anti-infidel rhetoric that sometimes comes from their mosques and that pollutes some of their textbooks.

The Education System

What is clearer is that there is one place where, without question, the power of the clerics in Saudi Arabia is a problem, and that's in the schools. And that problem, in turn, flows through the economy in ways that could, in the long run, be dangerous. Simply put, one of the ways in which the al Sauds have kept the conservative clerics happy is by allowing them to "hijack" the educational system, as one American businessman in Jiddah told me. "The education system has slipped here," concedes Prince Abdullah bin Faisal, CEO of the Saudi Arabian General Investment Authority, a key economic planning agency. "[The curriculum] has become classically and religiously oriented—and so out of touch." And why that matters leads directly to the economic conundrum in which the Saudis now find themselves.

If your image of Saudi Arabia is one of oil-rich sheikhs snapping up London townhouses, then a trip to the southwestern region of Asir will change that. Asir looks nothing like Riyadh. It is mountainous, and some of the small villages tucked into those mountains have been there for centuries. This is where some of the Sept. 11 hijackers were from, and by Saudi standards parts of Asir are downtrodden. Nationwide, per capita income in Saudi Arabia has plummeted, from a peak of $15,000 in 1981 to $7,700 in 2000, and it is places like the small villages outside of Abha that have felt it most. A young man I met in Asir did not want his name used, and it was clear why. He was openly critical of the royal family's profligate spending in an era when he and many of his peers are struggling. Like an increasing number of young Saudi men, he graduated recently from an Islamic studies program at a university, and now finds himself without a job. He has no technical skills and no particular interest in business. And menial work—waiting tables or construction jobs—is still mainly done by the five million foreign workers in the kingdom. Though some Saudis now toil in grocery stores or in other relatively low-paying service positions, too many, including the one I met in Asir, consider that kind of work beneath them.

In the mid-1980s, Saudi Arabia sent 12,500 students abroad annually to study. With the increase in the number of universities in the country, just 3,000 students received their degrees overseas in 2000. A great many more Saudis now attend university, but the problem, to hear employers talk, is that many of these homegrown institutions are dominated by conservative clerics, and they are turning out young men (to the extent that women in Saudi Arabia work, they tend to be nurses and teachers) who are not equipped for the modern workplace. As the businessman in Jiddah puts it, "These guys know Allah but not algorithms."

That matters, because the Saudis are once again learning that their dependence on oil is a problem. Oil revenue accounts for 75% of the nation's budget, 40% of its Gross Domestic Product (GDP), and 90% of its export revenue. After the demand for oil surged during the booming 1990s, the country is now back to reality: Demand is slumping, and Oil Minister Al Naimi, the most powerful figure within the Organization of Petroleum Exporting Countries (OPEC), is struggling to get the increasingly important non-OPEC producers like Russia to cut production. The result: Oil prices have plunged to a two-year low amid the global recession.

For the Saudis, the message is clear: They need to diversify their economic base in a hurry. If there ever was an era when the average Saudi really was so rich that when the Mercedes ran out of gas he just left it at the side of the road and bought a new one, it's long, long gone. A faintly comical remnant of that fairy-tale era is that the kingdom itself does not keep unemployment statistics. But Brad Bourland, the chief economist at the Saudi American Bank, estimates unemployment at no less than 20% of a work force that is overwhelmingly young.

It is here that the outlines of a nightmare scenario for the kingdom become visible. A generation of young men, already (by dint of their educations) more influenced than their predecessors were by fundamentalist clerics, find themselves unemployable. The royal family carries on with its legendarily lavish lifestyle. (One of King Fahd's sons recently built a palace in Riyadh modeled after the Alhambra, the Spanish castle.) Maybe a split develops within the House of Saud, between those (like Crown Prince Abdullah) who want to rein in the corruption and those who want the status quo. The *ulema* chooses sides. Is unrest out of the question? Is there not an "Iran" scenario out there somewhere?

If there is, we are still a long way from it. The government has taken some first, albeit fairly feeble, steps toward economic reform. Despite the fierce protests of the national oil and gas monopoly, Saudi Aramco, the government will allow Exxon, Mobil and Shell to drill for natural gas in three separate regions—a signal that the Saudis are serious about attracting more foreign direct investment. On Dec. 16, 2001, the companies were expected to sign an agreement with the government nailing down the terms of the deal, which should allow the drilling to begin sometime in 2002. The government is also mulling what is, by Saudi standards, a fairly ambitious privatization schedule, hoping to sell off pieces of state-owned monopolies in telecommunications, power generation, and aviation. That could help ameliorate budget problems that have become chronic. If anything, says one Western diplomat, the economic slump could hasten the reform process, " because it illustrates there is no other way for them to go."

There are also three important facts to keep in mind about potential "crisis" scenarios in Saudi Arabia. One is that, for all the talk about the kingdom's economic problems, the level of poverty in the Shah's Iran was far greater than anything in the kingdom today. Two: The House of Saud and the clerics have effectively co-opted each other, so a massive Khomeini-like challenge to the ruling order seems unlikely, particularly since the ruling family still retains deep reservoirs of respect within the Saudi population and has withstood crises, both internal and external, before. Who remembers today that in 1975 King Faisal was assassinated by his nephew?

And finally, there is all that oil. Yes, other folks have a lot too, but no one can produce it more cheaply than the Saudis, and that is a lesson they are once again teaching the other producers: A price war is the oil-patch equivalent of a contest to see who can hold his breath the longest. Those contests are painful for the Saudis—but much more painful for the rest of the world's producers. It's that geology again.

Saudi Arabia Commits Human Rights Abuses

By Human Rights Watch

Human Rights Watch (HRW) is an organization that monitors and publishes reports on human rights conditions worldwide. The following selection was excerpted from the Saudi Arabia section of its World Report 2003, *which documents the status of human rights in 2002. HRW concludes that despite the introduction of a new criminal code, the Saudi Arabian justice system continues to employ torture, falsely imprison suspects, and hold secret trials. In addition, the government restricts free expression by the press and women's rights organizations; forbids women to drive, work in certain occupations, or marry non-Muslims; and discriminates against religious minority groups.*

Following the attacks on New York and Washington on September 11, 2001, Saudi Arabia faced the most sustained international scrutiny in its modern history. Despite massive media attention and liberal access granted to Western journalists, detailed information about human rights violations remained elusive. The continuing absence of a local human rights movement and the government's policy of keeping the kingdom closed to investigators from international human rights organizations contributed to the information shortage, as did the Interior Ministry's effective use of harassment and intimidation to keep human rights victims and their advocates silent. Interior Ministry operatives also pressured families of perceived critics and in several documented cases security officials detained close relatives without charge.

Human Rights Developments

The broad features of the kingdom's human rights landscape remained unchanged. Saudi Arabia lacked independent national institutions to question, criticize or hold accountable the all-powerful executive branch of government controlled by the royal family. The appointed Consultative Council (majlis al-shura) had a limited role and was no substitute for an elected parliament with independent oversight powers. Political groups of any kind were not permitted and demonstrations were banned. Meetings and public assemblies required permission of the authorities. Procedures to obtain legal status for nongovernmental organizations (NGOs) remained cumbersome and opaque, with independent groups unable to establish themselves. The department of statistics disclosed on August 9 [2002] that 50 percent of the Saudi population was under the age of fifteen. It remained unclear how authorities were prepared to accommodate this educated and potentially restive population in the coming years, since students were not permitted to organize groups to articulate their concerns.

Freedom of expression, including press freedom, was limited, and authorities took punitive measures against journalists and others viewed as too outspoken. The King Abdul Aziz Center for Science and Technology controlled access to the Internet. Users were unable to reach sites that authorities blocked for political or "moral" reasons. There were no independent women's rights organizations to give voice to gender issues, such as discrimination in the legal and education systems and sharp restrictions on women's freedom of movement. Similarly, the kingdom had no NGOs to advocate for the rights of religious minorities—notably, Shiite and Ismaili Muslims who faced serious discrimination—or the kingdom's estimated six million to seven million foreign workers. Senior government officials refused to give credence to reports of human rights violations and reacted defensively when such information was publicized internationally.

The New Code of Criminal Procedure

On the positive side, the newly adopted code of criminal procedure came into force on May 1 [2002]. The law represented an important step toward greater transparency in the administration of the criminal justice system by specifying legal procedures and due-process rights. Notably, it prohibited torture and other forms of ill treatment, stated clearly that persons arrested or detained must be promptly informed of the charges against them, and acknowledged the right of criminal suspects to the assistance of lawyers during investigation proceedings and trial. It also provided for oversight of prisons and other places of detention by members of the Public Investigation and Prosecution Department to ensure that no one was detained or imprisoned in an unlawful manner.

Some of the code's provisions were at odds with international human rights standards, such as article 33, which stated that suspects must establish their innocence to the satisfaction of non-judicial authorities within the first twenty-four hours of arrest or face the prospect of long-term detention. Despite the code's various deficiencies, it nevertheless provided important benchmarks for assessing the practices of internal security and police forces, public prosecutors, and other officials. But without an active network of human rights lawyers or an effective civil rights association serving citizens and foreign residents alike, it remained to be seen how compliance with the code will be monitored and how violations of it will be addressed. It also remained unclear how the government planned to educate the public about the new law. Saudi citizens interviewed by Human Rights Watch during the year had no knowledge of the code or the specific rights it guaranteed.

Bombings and Torture

Westerners continued to be targeted and killed in mysterious car bombings, which the government maintained were not the work of Saudis. On June 20 [2002], British banker Simon Veness died in Riyadh when his car exploded on the way to work. Nine days later, also in Riyadh, an American couple discovered a bomb under their car before it detonated. On September 29, German worker W. Maximilian Graf was killed in Riyadh when his car exploded. Prince Nawwaf bin Abdulaziz, director of the General Intelligence Department, called it an "isolated" incident and not "a terrorist [act] against foreigners in the kingdom."

Torture under interrogation of political prisoners and criminal suspects continued. One Saudi prisoner, released in 2002 after being held for six years without charge or trial by the Interior Ministry's General Directorate of Investigation (popularly called *mabahith* in Arabic), said that as a condition of release he was forced to sign a pledge that he would not speak or write to anyone about what he witnessed. In a document provided to Human Rights Watch he described how detainees were tortured, including "beating with sticks, whips, and electric cables; use of a revolving electric chair until the victim loses consciousness and begins to vomit; sleep deprivation for long periods, up to one week; and forcing the victim to stand on one leg and raise one arm for extended periods." He also alleged that prisoners were subjected to "sexual harassment by threat or the actual practice [of] inserting an iron rod in the rectum," and held in "solitary confinement for more than four months, in some cases in a windowless room less than two meters square and without ventilation." Human Rights Watch also received credible information concerning the physical and psychological torture meted out to five Britons and one Canadian imprisoned as suspects in bombings of Westerners that began in November 2000. Techniques included: continuous sleep deprivation for up to ten days; abrupt slapping on the face and punches to the body; forcing them to stand while their hands were shackled to the top of a door; hanging them upside down, with their hands and feet shackled; and threats to harm their relatives if they did not agree to sign dictated confessions.

In September [2002], British citizen Ron Jones, a forty-nine-year-old accountant, initiated legal action to sue the Saudi government for false imprisonment and torture during his sixty-seven days of detention in 2001. He was injured in a bombing in Riyadh in March 2001; within twenty-four hours Jones was removed from his hospital bed and detained by the Interior Ministry as a suspect, according to *The Guardian* (London). "They said they knew I was part of the bombing circle, that I had planted the bomb, and that if I didn't admit it they would torture me until I confessed," Jones told the newspaper.

Secret and Irregular Trials

Secret and wholly irregular trials of Saudis and foreigners continued. In some cases, it appeared that the defendants themselves were not aware that a trial was in progress, since they were asked to do no more than verify that a signed confession was their own. In February, Prince Nayef said that the case of seven foreigners—five Britons, one Canadian, and one Belgian charged with the anti-Western bombings—was "before the judiciary." He provided no additional details. Human Rights Watch learned that the defendants were secretly tried and sentenced without the notification or presence of their Saudi defense lawyers. Nor were the lawyers informed when the Court of Cassation and the Supreme Judicial Council (SJC) reviewed and approved the sentences—reportedly eight years for Belgian Raf Schyvens, eighteen years for Britons Pete Brandon, James Cottle, James Lee, and Les Walker, and the death penalty for Briton Alexander Mitchell and Canadian William Sampson. In a special written appeal to the SJC after it upheld the sentences, the lawyers made clear that they had no opportunity to defend their clients while the legal proceedings were underway; that the only evidence presented was coerced confessions obtained under torture; and that judges ignored defendants' claims of coerced confessions and did not request in-vestigations. The lawyers also pointed out that similar car bombings of Westerners continued after the arrest of their clients, citing the June 20 attack that killed a Briton in Riyadh.

Deputy Interior Minister Prince Ahmed bin Abdulaziz revealed on June 13 that some of the suspects in the 1996 bombing of the Khobar Towers, in which 19 U.S. Air Force personnel were killed, were tried in a court of first instance. He did not disclose the dates of the trial or the names or number of defendants. He provided few details other than that the group "did not include non-Saudi nationals." The prince said the "sentences will go to a higher court, then to the Supreme Judicial Council and then to the king for approval," adding vaguely that the verdicts would be "announced at the appropriate time.". . .

The Rights of Women and Girls

The rights of Saudi women and girls remained captive to the kingdom's patriarchal social-cultural traditions as well as conservative interpretations of *shari'a* (Islamic law). Women did not enjoy freedom of movement and required permission from their fathers, husbands, or other close male relatives to travel inside the kingdom or abroad. Some 3,500 members of the Committee to Promote Virtue and Prevent Vice, or religious police, enforced the mandatory dress code for women. In May [2002], the Commerce Ministry confirmed that it was coordinating with the religious police to clamp down on local factories that made *abayas* (the traditional formless black cloaks that were regulation public attire for Saudi women) that officials considered risqué. The garments were reportedly becoming popular in some Saudi cities. Authorities were prepared to confiscate and destroy the new abayas and take "punitive measures" against their owners, according to a May 2 story in *Arab News*.

The ongoing ban on women driving caused economic hardship in some families and tremendous inconvenience for young graduates of teacher colleges assigned to schools in outlying districts. The government began in November 2001 to issue photo identification cards to women for the first time, although it did so "very quietly without any publicity in the press or the state-run radio and TV," Agence France-Presse reported on December 2, 2001. Women reportedly required the written permission of a spouse or other male guardian to obtain the cards. Some Saudi women dismissed the move as "window dressing" for the West, making no real difference in their lives. "You still need your husband's or male guardian's permission to apply for a job, be admitted to a hospital, and travel anywhere inside or abroad. Without their approval, you cannot do anything," one Riyadh-based educated mother of three told Human Rights Watch. The national pol-

icy of gender segregation limited education and employment opportunities for women and girls, although they were enrolled in numbers
proportionate to men and boys at all levels of the education system,
including universities. Women were not permitted to study engineer-
ing and were barred from attending the prestigious King Fahd University of Petroleum and Minerals, which trained a male student body
of some seven thousand for jobs in the energy industry.

Blatant gender discrimination meant that Saudi women and girls
(Saudi law sets no minimum age for marriage) were not permitted to
marry non-Muslims and could not pass on their Saudi citizenship to
their children from non-Saudi fathers. Foreigners married to or di-
vorced from Saudi men faced an added discriminatory burden: They
were not permitted to enter the kingdom to visit their children without the written permission of the fathers, who had to file a "statement
of no objection" with the Interior Ministry as a condition for granting a visa, according to the U.S. State Department January 2002 report on international parental child abduction.

The tragic fire at an overcrowded and unsafe public school for
girls in Mecca on March 11 [2002], in which fifteen were killed, pre-
cipitated a public uproar in the kingdom and unprecedented critical
press coverage of the religious police and the General Presidency for
Girls Education (GPGE), the conservative agency responsible for
policymaking and administration of female education. A March 25
royal decree forced GPGE head Ali bin Murshid al-Murshid into
early retirement and merged the GPGE with the Ministry of Education, ending its historic autonomy. But senior government officials
appeared reluctant to take on the religious police, whom eyewitnesses
criticized for hampering rescue efforts at the school because the fleeing girls were not properly attired in the customary abayas and head
coverings. On March 24, Interior Minister Prince Nayef implicitly
defended the religious police, stating: "The fire was extinguished by
the civil defence [force] within five minutes." He then criticized the
Saudi press for inaccurate reporting: "Have those who reported the
incident been competent and responsible? Sorrowfully no. Every correspondent wanted to satisfy his newspaper [by] exaggerating." On
April 9, Prince Saud bin Fahd, deputy chief of intelligence, said: "In-
vestigations into the fire incident proved that the [religious police]
had done nothing wrong."

Press Restrictions
The public controversy surrounding the Mecca fire had broader im-
plications for the local press. Prince Nayef met with newspaper edi-
tors and "scolded them for crossing lines concerning religion," the

Associated Press reported from Riyadh on April 24, citing a source who attended the meeting. This informal control of the press from the top, influencing coverage and content, was noted by Saudi journalism professor Suleiman al-Shammari, whom the Associated Press quoted as saying: "The government acts like the media's doorman, especially when it comes to foreign policy, opening and closing the door when it wishes."

Muhamed Mukhtar al-Fal, editor in chief of the daily *al-Madina,* was dismissed from his post in March, reportedly on orders of the interior minister. The action came after the newspaper published "The Corrupt on Earth," a poem of Saudi writer and poet Abdel Mohsen Mosallam. The poem lambasted corrupt judges, stating in part: "Your beards are smeared with blood. You indulge a thousand tyrants and only the tyrant do you obey." Mosallam was arrested on March 18, eight days after the newspaper published his poem. He was held for eighteen days without charge in a mubahith office in Riyadh and was not mistreated during his detention. As of this writing, he was blacklisted, unable to publish in Saudi newspapers, and banned from traveling. Al-Fal was not reinstated to his post but was not banned from writing.

Discrimination Against Religious Minorities

The government did not respect the rights of religious minorities in the kingdom, whether these communities were Saudi or expatriate. In April 2000, Ismaili Shiite Muslims in the southern province of Najran protested the storming and closure of a mosque, leading to violent clashes with Saudi security forces and mass arrests. In December 2001, Ismaili elders in Najran issued a public statement, charging that ninety-three Ismailis remained imprisoned and seventeen of them faced the death penalty, adding that they were being held "for opposing the condition of degradation, repression and humiliation that is practiced against them and their tribesmen by Saudi authorities because of their faith." Subsequent unconfirmed reports said the death sentences had been commuted to life imprisonment. On January 9, 2002, the *Wall Street Journal* published an article from Najran discussing discrimination against the Ismaili minority. It quoted tribal leader Sheikh Ahmed Turki al-Sa'ab, who said: "We love our country, but we believe that the government is making a mistake against us." Although this was his only quote in the article, he was reportedly arrested on January 15 and on April 23 sentenced to seven years imprisonment and flogging. On February 25, the *Wall Street Journal* reported that two other Ismaili tribal leaders, Sheikh Hamad Ali Daseeny, a retired geologist, and Hamad Qulayyan al-Zbaidy, had been detained on February 4.

Members of the kingdom's Shi'a Muslim minority, numbering about one million—six percent of the Saudi population—continued to assert that the government practiced severe forms of discrimination against them, including toleration of hate speech from the pulpits of Sunni Muslim mosques and from educators in public schools. The Interior Ministry targeted outspoken peaceful critics, harassed them in interrogation sessions, and threatened them with sanctions including loss of their jobs.

Christian residents of the kingdom were not permitted any public display of their faith. The government did not allow churches of any Christian denomination to occupy public space, in sharp contrast to the large number of churches allowed in nearby Dubai. Asian and African Christians suspected of proselytizing Saudi Muslims were arrested and imprisoned in harsh conditions, and pressured to convert to Islam as a condition of release. Two U.S.-based groups, International Christian Concern and Middle East Concern, publicized the arrest and detention between July and September 2001 in Jeddah of eleven foreign nationals—from India, Eritrea, Ethiopia, and the Philippines. They reportedly were held for practicing their religion in their homes. One of them, Dennis Moreno-Lacalla, a Filipino who worked in the kingdom for sixteen years, was arrested in Jeddah in August 2001 and held without charge until his release seven months later. He said that he witnessed the flogging of three Ethiopian Christians—Tinsaie Gizachew, Bahru Menguistu, and Gebeyahu Tafera—in January 2002, reporting that the men were "kicked, suspended with chains, and lashed 80 times with a steel rod cable about one inch in diameter," punishment that left them bleeding and in severe pain.

The government took action to move the kingdom slightly closer to compliance with international labor standards when Minister of Labor and Social Affairs Dr. Ali al-Namlah authorized on April 17 the creation of "labor committees" at companies with one hundred or more employees, although foreign workers were barred from committee membership. International Labor Organization (ILO) Director General Juan Somavía described it as "a milestone in the labor history of Saudi Arabia." The ILO also reported that a second expert team completed consultations with the Labor Ministry in April concerning a new labor law, which it said would be submitted to the kingdom's appointed Consultative Council (majlis al-shura) "in the near future."

Despite this positive development, foreign workers in the kingdom—particularly Arabs and South Asians in low-wage occupations, including women domestic workers—remained extremely vulnerable to poor working conditions and other abuse at the hands of their employers, who typically held their passports and official residence permits (*iqama*, in Arabic). With these documents essentially confiscated, these workers had limited freedom of movement. They were unable to leave the country unless their employment sponsors requested an exit visa, and were subjected to arrest and steep fines if stopped without residence permits in their possession. Foreigner workers comprised about 65 percent of the private sector labor force, the U.S. State Department's Bureau of Economic and Business Affairs reported in February.

Defending Human Rights

The absence of freedom of association, coupled with strict limits on freedom of expression, left Saudi citizens and other residents of the kingdom without the ability to report openly about human rights conditions. There were no independent rights organizations, including women's rights groups, despite signing the Convention on the Elimination of All Forms of Discrimination Against Women (CEDAW) in 2000. The U.N. special rapporteur on the independence of judges and lawyers [Param Cumaraswamy], during an official mission to Saudi Arabia in October, reported that the government was "proposing the establishment of a national human rights institution."

Some Saudi citizens who suffered rights abuses, or collected information about such abuses, communicated to the outside world in clandestine fashion for fear of punishment at the hands of authorities. Human Rights Watch received information in 2002 from individuals who were summoned to the Interior Ministry and questioned at length about publicizing human rights abuses and contacting international human rights groups. Such harassment and intimidation enforced their silence, leaving them frightened and fearful of arrest or dismissal from their public-sector jobs.

The kingdom remained closed to international human rights organizations during the year. As of this writing, Saudi authorities did not respond to Human Rights Watch's longstanding requests to visit. Amnesty International was similarly denied. In December 2001, Lieutenant-General Ali Hussein al-Harithi, head of the Interior Ministry's General Directorate of Prisons, told al-Sharq al-Awsat newspaper that Amnesty International and other groups were welcome to visit at "any time." He added: "We have nothing to hide or fear. [They] will find that the reality of our prisons and inmates does not conform with what is rumored or said about them." A Human Rights Watch letter to the government following up on these remarks went unanswered.

Christians Must Promote Religious Freedom in Saudi Arabia

By Jeff M. Sellers

The official religion of Saudi Arabia is a form of Islam called Wahhabism, which advocates a very strict interpretation of the Koran and shariah *(Islamic law). According to many analysts, the Wahhabi interpretation of Islam in Saudi Arabia has produced one of the most repressive societies in the world. Jeff M. Sellers, an associate editor for* Christianity Today, *examines the role of the* mutawaa'in, *or religious police, and the Muslim clergy in Saudi society with regard to religious freedom. Despite efforts by political leaders to reform the religious establishment, Sellers argues that conservative elements in the clergy and the* mutawaa'in *are still persecuting Christians and other religious minorities. According to Sellers, the best way to remedy the problems of religious freedom and human rights in Saudi Arabia is to confront the Muslim clergy with Islamic scripture, which contains the legal and spiritual bases for a more tolerant Saudi society.*

Every year Saudi Arabia lands on or near the top of lists of violators of religious freedom, and every year the royal family that rules the kingdom could not care less. The United States has formed an alliance with this intransigent opponent of human rights for reasons that parallel the charge given to Lawrence of Arabia. Leading Saudi Arabia forward into unfathomable wealth by developing its oil industry, the United States has found the partnership profitable for both economic and geopolitical interests.

Jeff M. Sellers, "How to Confront a Theocracy," *Christianity Today*, vol. 46, July 8, 2002. Copyright © 2002 by Jeff M. Sellers. Reproduced by permission.

U.S. oil companies arrived in Saudi Arabia a generation after Lawrence helped lead Arabs in their revolt against World War I-era Turks. Like the Christians who often work for these and other companies, Lawrence had no illusions about the limits of his ability to assume Arab character. But he did defer to his host culture, accepting its ways as a point of departure, and his example in war may yet have something to teach us about spiritual battles for human dignity.

The Persecution of Wally Magdangal

In 1992, December 25 fell on a Friday, the Muslim day of rest, when pastor Oswaldo "Wally" Magdangal was to be hanged in the Saudi capital of Riyadh for blaspheming Islam. Shari'ah law requires beheading for "apostates"—those who renounce Islam—as well as for murderers, and no Friday passes without at least one such execution in the public square following the noon prayers, rights organizations say. Hangings are reserved for "blasphemers" like Magdangal. Foreigners of non-Islamic faiths can worship legally in private in Saudi Arabia, but the 42-year-old Filipino pastor was arrested after his growing house church had become too noticeable. On December 23, 1992, Magdangal wrote out his last will and testament for his wife and young daughter.

Religious police had tortured every part of his body in trying to force him to renounce his faith in Christ. Embracing Islam would have won his immediate release. Initially the religious police, or muttawa'in—a vigilante force with a hierarchy and membership extending into government and other sectors—beat him throughout 210 minutes of mocking interrogation. They handed him a pencil and paper and demanded names of other Christians he knew. He refused. . . .

During interrogations—which included flogging of his back, his palms, and the soles of his feet—the muttawa'in did not state charges against him. Only when he answered that he agreed with an article predicting the ultimate fall of Islam in *Christ for the Nations* magazine (which the muttawa'in found in his home) was the basis for the eventual blasphemy charge established.

Magdangal was not allowed to speak during his high court trial, which Muslim clerics held in secret.

"I was shaking with pain; I was trembling with fear," Magdangal says. "I kept asking them to get my wife, but that led them to tell me in strong words to stand silent—not to say a word or I would suffer the consequence of every word I spoke. That's when I just broke down, and I just wept and wept."

By then the lower court had read some charges—preaching a message different from the Qur'an, "building" a church—but only hinted at the blasphemy charge. Magdangal would learn of the blasphemy verdict before he knew the charge itself: a muttawa'in officer interrogating him, Lt. Bader Alyaya, said his case had become "very serious" and that he was going to be hanged.

"He motioned around his neck like a noose, and then he pulled the noose above his head in a motion with his hand," he recalls. "I knew that people guilty of blasphemy are hanged to death for three days, to send a strong warning to the Muslims not to turn to another religion, and for Christians to not try to reach the Muslims.". . .

Normally Saudi authorities do not tell the condemned of their sentence until the day of their execution, so as to forestall appeals and protests, Magdangal says. Sometimes the authorities go the extra step of leading prisoners to believe they are being released just before executing them.

Magdangal knew only that the Philippine embassy had filed protests of his detention, which went unheeded, though soon Amnesty International also was monitoring his case. As executive secretary to the Saudi director of Defense and Civil Aviation, Magdangal had close friends high in the Saudi government, including members of the royal family—and even in the muttawa'in—who only gradually had become aware of his arrest. Muttawa'in officers warned each of Magdangal's high-level friends to stop advocating for him.

The threats worked. But a general secretly told Magdangal's wife to inform Fidel Ramos, then-president of the Philippines, that the case had become "very serious."

"The reality is that in Saudi Arabia the majority of the people, even those in the government, are not aware that the Muslim clerics are persecuting Christians," Magdangal says. "Even among the Muslim clerics, not all of them are aware that some of their colleagues are persecuting Christians."

Fresh off victory from Saudi soil in the Gulf War, the U.S. Congress and the White House joined with human-rights organizations to appeal for Magdangal's life—unbeknownst to him. By December 23, 1992, he had settled in his heart that he was going to be executed. . . .

Magdangal prayed that if he were spared, he would be a voice for the persecuted. Shortly before midnight, the prison commander arrived with orders to deport Magdangal. "Even at that point, from the prison to the airport, I was very terrified because the two officers with me were interrupted on their radio by Muslim clerics who were yelling, fighting my release, and telling them to divert the car and bring it somewhere else to kill me," he says.

Now president of Christians in Crisis, an advocacy group based in

Sacramento, California, Magdangal later learned from a friend high in the muttawa'in that military advisers were vying with clerics for the ear of King Fahd bin Abdul al-Aziz Al Saud—whose mandate in Saudi Arabia, the clerics reminded him, was to uphold Shari'ah.

"The war was still very fresh, and Saddam Hussein was still a major threat," Magdangal recalls. "The military advisers were saying, in essence, 'King, we are under such pressure from the friendly nations—what is one person compared to what we are facing from Saddam Hussein, and all the benefits that might be diminished as a result of executing this person?'"

King Fahd ordered Magdangal to be expelled within 24 hours. According to Magdangal's muttawa'in contact, 500 Muslim clerics resigned their state posts in protest.

Religious Persecution After September 11

Magdangal believes the advent of U.S. sorties against Iraq in the Gulf War triggered a wavelet of Saudi persecution of Christians that led to his arrest. Islamic leaders, fearing closer ties with the United States would tighten the rein on them, decided to attack Christians while they could. They would not arrest him until months later, but muttawa'in raided Magdangal's house hours before U.S. bombing began.

A decade after the Gulf War, the U.S.-Saudi relationship is much more contentious as America pressures its key regional ally, largely in vain, for cooperation in the "war on terrorism"—and this as the two countries hold opposite allegiances in the Israeli-Palestinian conflict raging in the foreground of the Saudi conscience. It is virtually impossible to know what effect the convoluted and secretive U.S.-Saudi relationship might have on persecution levels in Saudi Arabia, but kingdom observers see signs that the royal family is steadily corralling the religious police.

Charles W. Freeman Jr., president of the Washington-based Middle East Policy Council, was U.S. Ambassador to Saudi Arabia during the Gulf War. He believes the uprightness of Crown Prince Abdullah bin Abd al-Aziz Al Saud, half-brother of the stroke-impaired King Fahd and to some extent the de facto ruler, will favorably influence the muttawa'in.

"Particularly under Crown Prince Abdullah, the muttawa'in are very much subdued and on the defensive," Freeman says. "And one of the reasons he's able to rein in some of the more fanatical elements of the Saudi populace is that he himself has a well-justified reputation for being a pious and godly man."

The government recently struck a blow to the clerics following a March 11, 2002, fire at a girls' public intermediate school in Mecca. As 835 students and 55 women teachers fled the building, several members of the muttawa'in beat them back because they were not wearing their long black cloaks and head coverings. They also beat civil defense workers trying to rescue the girls.

This interference reportedly caused some of the 14 casualties. The government not only fired the head of the General Presidency for Girls' Education—a powerful institution controlled by the clerics—but also abolished it in function. The regime folded it into the Ministry of Education, according to Virginia Sherry, associate director of the Middle East Division of Human Rights Watch.

In addition, since September 11 the Saudi government has instructed clerics to preach a more tolerant version of Islam, Sherry notes. "There's speculation as to whether or not that's posturing for a Western audience, but it's also clearly intended to rein in the clerics," she says.

Freeman, who has also been assistant secretary of defense for international security affairs, says Abdullah is trying to find ways to open the kingdom and make it more tolerant, even in the area of religion.

"Certainly the discovery that Osama bin Laden was able to recruit Saudis to his cause—his cause being to overthrow the Saudi monarchy, with the attack on the United States being merely a means to that end—actually set off quite a bit of soul-searching in the kingdom," Freeman says.

A slight easing of religious intolerance could emerge from such reflection, both Freeman and Sherry say. Freeman notes that Abdullah has considered allowing Christian organizations with medical programs to help attend to the thousands of wounded Palestinians who are treated in Saudi Arabia. And he calls a speech that Abdullah gave to the Gulf Cooperation Council in December 2001 "very remarkable, because it reflects a spirit of soul-searching and self-criticism that is not too often seen among leaders anywhere, much less in the Arab world."

Whether such setbacks for the muttawa'in make them more dangerous or less to underground churches in Saudi Arabia is a murky matter. Traditionally, such cornering of the religious animal can cause the muttawa'in to strike with more ferocity.

"The religious authorities and their police force are putting constant pressure on the civil authorities to be more Islamic—including to act stronger against Christian activity," says one rights advocate based in the United Kingdom. "At the moment, and as a result of

September 11, the government is more vulnerable to pressure from the religious elements."

The Power of Muslim Clerics in Saudi Arabia

The clerics' power—including the leverage to topple the government—cannot be discounted. In the royal family's precarious position between the forces of modernity and traditional clerics, Saudi rulers generally have tried to appease religious dissidents rather than clamp down too severely, says Dudley Woodberry, a pastor in Riyadh in 1976–79 and dean emeritus and professor of Islamic Studies at Fuller Theological Seminary.

Indeed, *The New Yorker* reported in its October 22, 2001, edition that electronic intercepts of conversations in the royal family show the regime is so insecure that it has funneled hundreds of millions of dollars in "protection money" to fundamentalist groups that would otherwise overthrow it. Some of the Saudi funds went to Osama bin Laden's Al Qaeda group, according to the report.

"The dilemma one faces," said Ambassador Freeman, "is that those who are most opposed to the royal family are either themselves murderers, that is, morally depraved people, or they resemble the followers of the late Ayatollah Khomeini in their vision of a future that is even less tolerant than the prevailing one. That is, the dissidents who are sitting in London are not arguing for a more open and tolerant society; they're arguing the opposite, as Khomeini turned out to do for Iran."

With restive, unemployed youth stuck in a cracked economy increasingly filling their ranks, Saudi extremist groups could lash out at the 870,000 Christians among the country's 7 million foreign workers (nearly a third of the country's population). If the response of a Saudi underground church to queries by *Christianity Today* is any indication, fear still weighs heavily in the atmosphere—all members felt answering questions could jeopardize their safety. One Western man daring to reply anyway said that since 1998, the Christian community has been through several periods of arrest, detention, and deportation of leaders.

"Most of those began with Christians being 'too visible,'" he told *CT*. "These have been almost entirely Asians, and they pay the greatest price in terms of lost leadership, loss of income, and harassment from employers and religious authorities. Quite honestly, I do not want to answer your questions. Am I being overly cautious or gun-shy? I don't know."

Concerned that descriptions of his life in Saudi Arabia would provoke a crackdown, the Westerner nevertheless said he hoped this article would "inform Christians about the intolerant, close-minded attitude of Saudi Arabia and much of the Muslim world. Christians need to know this."

The U.S. Commission on International Religious Freedom knew this well, recommending—unsuccessfully, given obvious diplomatic sensitivities—that the State Department designate Saudi Arabia as one of nine "countries of particular concern." The commission dismissed the Saudi claim that non-Muslims are permitted private worship. The Saudi definition of "private worship" is vague, and underground worshipers have been "arrested, imprisoned, deported and harassed by the authorities," according to the commission.

Appealing to Muslim Roots to Change Saudi Society

Saudi Arabia tops the lists of religious freedom violators for the same reason its rulers don't care about such lists: In a theocracy entrusted with preserving a narrow Islamic "purity" and the shrines in Mecca and Medina, denial of religious freedom is integral to the country's cultural identity. As Crown Prince Abdullah has said, the two holy shrines are the "primary restrictions" on change. "Our faith and our culture are what drive the country," he once said. Somehow, though, other Islamic countries have cultures far more tolerant than Saudi Arabia's.

Saudi Arabia is a charter member of the United Nations, and yet it brazenly disregards the U.N. Universal Declaration of Human Rights, which asserts the right to profess, propagate, and change faith. But U.N. ideals may not be the best starting point for transforming a medieval theocracy.

Saudi Arabia was founded on the Muslim equivalent of the Reformation—Wahhabism, which in the 1700s rejected the religious accretions of previous centuries to return to the authority of the Qur'an. Shari'ah is its constitution. Whereas the Christian Reformation eventually encouraged the separation of church and state, Saudi Arabia grew out of an alliance in 1744 between the political emir, Muhammad ibn Saud, and the Islamic reformer, Muhammad ibn Abd al Wahhab.

With religion and the state thus wedded, the U.N. Universal Declaration of Human Rights carries about as much weight in Saudi Arabia as a treatise on secular humanism would for conservative televangelists, Middle East observers say. Rather than start with institutions and documents that are Western in essence, it is better to address Saudis on their own terms—Islam's historical writings. Letters attributed to Muhammad in the Tabaqat of 9th-century historian Ibn Sa'd, for example, allowed Christians in Najran (in today's southwestern Saudi Arabia) to have churches and priests. Fuller Seminary's Woodberry used to distribute copies of these letters while pastor of a house church in Riyadh.

"We circulated these letters basically to let the government know that at least Muhammad had allowed the Christians that were in the area to continue to worship and have priests as long as they were loyal citizens," Woodberry says.

Avoiding the unenviable position of trying to interpret Islam for Saudis, church members limited themselves to passing out copies of the letters.

"We did it first in English, and then I gave them Arabic copies as well," Woodberry says. "It uses the sources that are considered important to them."

Likewise, the Qur'an says Jews and Christians belong to a category of people protected from aggression. Some references in the Qur'an also suggest that the Sabeans, probably a gnostic group in south Arabia, were also protected people, Woodberry says. That extra category has enabled the government of Indonesia, for example, to protect the religious freedom of Hindus and Buddhists. And there is a plethora of history in which Islam peacefully coexists with other faiths.

How do such Islamic documents go over with those of the strict Wahhabi faith? "Wahhabism emphasizes going back to the original sources of the faith, the Qur'an and Muhammad, so it's very impressive to them if you can point out that Muhammad allowed the Christians the freedom to raise their children as Christians, and to have churches and priests," Woodberry says.

He does not dismiss appeals to the U.N. charter. But any international pressure, Middle East observers say, must be applied gently in light of the Muslim clerics' fury at the generally corrupt regime seen as too friendly to the United States. "We never felt that the royal leadership was that much against us, but their position was tenuous enough that they didn't want the same thing to happen to them that had happened to Iran when the Shah was overthrown," Woodberry says.

Ambassador Freeman also suggests appeals to the human rights inherent in Islam. He notes that the Qur'anic injunction to submit to Allah presupposes choice and liberty of conscience, and that "Islam is very clear that there can be no compulsion in religion.". . .

Freeman holds out hope that, with some loosening of religious controls, Christians could earn the right through social service ministries to be heard about human rights. "It might be that an offer by a Christian church not to proselytize in Saudi Arabia, but to inspire by example, to minister to those who are maimed in the intifada by the Israeli occupation, might be timely," Freeman says.

This indirect route, compared with direct protest, is a quieter, more concealed, less conspicuous influence. Supporting Abdullah's efforts to gain entry into the World Trade Organization, thereby opening Saudi Arabia to more outside influences, would be another way of indirectly promoting human-rights issues, Freeman adds.

There is, however, a place for overt protest. Though the effects of agitating for human rights are disputed—sometimes they result in more severe persecution—in the long term, it is usually helpful that rogue regimes know the international community is watching. . . .

The Spiritual Basis for Confronting Religious Persecution

By appealing to Saudi sources of authority and offering to serve in their social causes, Western Christians might make the Saudis' struggle our struggle. That would entail finding a spiritual basis of mutual interest as powerful as the mundane one of oil for security. It also may mean identifying a common enemy—the Devil, as Magdangal prayed before he was to be hanged—rather than labeling each other as Satan. It's a lofty undertaking, but David E. Long, a former counter-terrorism official and author of *The Kingdom of Saudi Arabia*, notes that jihad has to do mainly with spiritual struggle.

"Jihad is the suppression of vice, maybe by force, and the encouragement of virtue, maybe by the sword, but nevertheless it's a broader concept," he says. "There's enough in Islam that is parallel and compatible with human rights that we could say, okay, fine, if you look at everything by Islamic law, but we encourage you to look at the human rights elements in Islam—after all, this is 'God's word.'"

Saudi Arabia Is Committed to the Cause of Universal Human Rights

By Torki Mohammed Saud Al-Kabeer

Several international organizations have identified Saudi Arabia as a violator of international human rights treaties. Among the violations that are commonly cited are a failure to guarantee freedom of religion, the equal rights of women, and the right to independent counsel in criminal court cases. In the following excerpt from his statements at the fifty-sixth session of the United Nations Commission on Human Rights in April 2000, Saudi prince Torki Mohammed Saud Al-Kabeer answers some of the criticism and asserts Saudi Arabia's support for universal human rights. The prince, who is also the undersecretary of political affairs and the director-general for the International Organizations department in Saudi Arabia, cites efforts to reform the Saudi judicial system and its "open door policy," which allows Saudi citizens to petition the king for a redress of grievances, as evidence of Saudi Arabia's commitment to the protection of human rights. The prince also argues that non-Muslim members of the international community have misrepresented the problems associated with Islamic law in Saudi Arabia and calls for a more open dialogue between Western and Islamic countries on the issue of human rights.

M r. Chairman:
I have the honor to address you, on behalf of the delegation of the Kingdom of Saudi Arabia, from this august rostrum on the important occasion of our annual gathering in which States with dif-

Torki Mohammed Saud Al-Kabeer, statement before the fifty-sixth session of the United Nations Commission on Human Rights, Geneva, April 6, 2000.

ferent cultures and civilizations meet in an endeavor to promote and protect human rights. In other words, the purpose of this important forum is to honor, and enhance the status of, the human person, whom God created and exalted. Successive ages have witnessed manifestations of man's injustice to his fellow man, illustrated by slavery, displacement and violation of his fundamental rights and human dignity.

We are happy to welcome the third millennium and begin it in a new and more promising manner conducive to optimism and hope, with unanimous agreement that human rights are a non-negotiable objective for the achievement of which we must all strive together.

My delegation looks forward to a successful session, under your wise direction, characterized by in-depth dialogue and exchanges of views, mutual trust and transparency in our work. Our common goal should be a joint endeavor to protect and defend human rights in a manner consistent with the aspirations of all. The broad and high-level international participation in this forum that we are attending today clearly proves the existence of a universal desire to promote closer international cooperation and a deeper understanding of all human rights issues. It also provides an opportunity to enrich the debate and the exchange of viewpoints concerning the various issues in an objective, equitable and balanced manner within a framework of mutual understanding, taking into account the constructive and effective way in which various civilizations and cultures are helping to enrich the concepts of human rights.

Mr. Chairman:

The rapidly growing concern for human rights has reached an advanced stage, as illustrated by the creation of a number of United Nations mechanisms and the establishment of many human rights bodies. This can be clearly perceived during the meetings and debates of the Commission on Human Rights, which play a major role in reconciling viewpoints and increasing the effectiveness of the work of its mechanisms in an atmosphere of mutual cooperation in which account is taken of the need to benefit from achievements of various civilizations and cultures in order to promote and enrich the process of the realization of human rights.

We in the Kingdom of Saudi Arabia welcome the role of these mechanisms, as well as the endeavors that are being made by the bodies and organizations concerned, and the international instruments to which they have given rise. However, in spite of these positive developments over the last fifty years, we find that grave violations of human rights are still being committed in many parts of the world. Consequently, there is a need for active endeavors to enrich the concepts of human rights by benefiting from the humanitarian values enshrined in the various religions, civilizations and cultures with a view to enhancing human life and providing a decent human environment. The noble and lofty principles advocated by these cultures could develop and preserve those concepts. Islam, like other religions, is unquestionably playing a leading role in this regard since it has helped, and is still helping, to enrich the concepts of human rights through its noble moral values and principles and its comprehensive way of life in which rights and obligations are defined in a just and equitable manner.

On this basis, the Kingdom of Saudi Arabia and the other States members of the Organization of the Islamic Conference are jointly seeking to promote the universality of human rights. Ten years after the adoption in 1990 of the Cairo Declaration on Human Rights, in response to the appeal to enrich the universality of human rights through agreements promoting regional cooperation, the Organization of the Islamic Conference adopted a resolution calling for the drafting of Islamic human rights instruments to supplement and support international endeavors in this field. These instruments will emphasize the need to protect individual and collective rights.

This step at the regional level is being accompanied by diligent endeavors at the domestic level. The Kingdom has made outstanding achievements and is looking forward to further ongoing improvement through its concern for human rights.

In addition to cooperating with this distinguished Commission, in early 2000 the Kingdom duly notified the UN special rapporteur on the independence of judges and lawyers that it would welcome a visit by him.

The Kingdom's support for human rights issues is not confined to their moral aspects; it includes financial support as the Kingdom has contributed to a number of voluntary funds established by the UN Office of the High Commissioner for Human Rights. The most recent contribution was made to the Plan of Action for the Convention on the Rights of the Child, which the Kingdom will continue to support.

In fulfillment of its obligations following its accession to the Convention Against Torture, the Kingdom established a committee consisting of various governmental bodies to investigate allegations of torture and other individual abuses.

The public are being made more aware of their human rights through the inclusion of these rights in educational curricula and media programs and emphasis is being placed on the need to apply humanitarian principles and values. . . .

In addition to the above, it is noteworthy that the regulations currently in force in the Kingdom of Saudi Arabia grant equal rights to citizens and foreign residents. They do not prohibit exercise of freedom of expression and assembly provided that this is neither prejudicial to public order nor detrimental to public morals. There are numerous channels through which individuals can express their opinion in full freedom in accordance with the so-called "open door policy", which means that, in keeping with the longstanding tradition, all State officials have an obligation to receive citizens and others, listen to their opinions and complaints and endeavor to find appropriate solutions to their problems. There are dozens of governmental and non-governmental bodies which engage in charitable and social activities and receive public support and assistance. In this context, tolerance, including religious tolerance, is a fundamental requirement for the achievement of more effective protection of human rights. We in the Kingdom of Saudi Arabia attach great importance to the principle of tolerance. The Kingdom has responded to the special rapporteur on religious intolerance who, in turn, thanked the Kingdom for its cooperation in this regard. Non-Muslim as well as all Muslim residents of the Kingdom enjoy all the basic rights and freedoms guaranteed to them in the relevant articles of the Basic System of Government.

In fact, non-Muslims enjoy full freedom to engage in their religious observances in private. No non-Muslims have ever been subjected to prosecution or punishment because of their religious faith and it is a punishable offence to subject them to any interference or harassments. . . .

In this connection, I wish to assure this distinguished Commission that all the Kingdom's laws and regulations apply to both sexes without distinction or exception. The Islamic *Shari'a* does not discriminate between men and women in regard to their duties and obligations. In fact, in accordance with the Convention on the Elimination of All Forms of Racial Discrimination to which the Kingdom has acceded, its regulations strictly prohibit all forms of discriminatory practices and the competent authorities in the Kingdom are endeavoring to ensure that women enjoy all their legally recognized rights, such as the right to work, the right to health care and social welfare, the right to protection from poverty and the right to free education at all levels. The educational enrolment rate among girls amounts to 95 per cent, which is equivalent to the rate among boys. Moreover, the female illiteracy rate has declined sharply to 15 per cent and we are endeavoring to reduce this rate to the lowest possible level. The State also provides stipends and appropriate accommodation for female students in a manner consistent with their basic needs. Educational expenditure accounts for 25 per cent of the State's budget, which is one of the world's highest proportions and represents 9 per cent of GNP. These figures clearly demonstrate the concern that my country's Government is showing for education, and especially female education, since it constitutes the cornerstone for the advancement and development of society.

Mr. Chairman:

We are surprised and concerned to note that some members of the international community find it hard to understand human rights in Islam or have difficulty in accepting the particularities that characterize Islamic and other societies. In some cases, the failure to convey the true concept of human rights in Islam might be attributable to the lack or inadequacy of intercultural dialogue. However, this does not give anyone the right to defame any principles or values that seek to promote the advancement of mankind and preserve human dignity and rights. At the same time, we welcome constructive dialogue among the various civilizations and cultures with a view to ensuring protection of the human person and human rights. . . .

In conclusion, Mr. Chairman, I wish to assure you of my Government's support for your commendable endeavors to achieve the noble aims and objectives of the promotion of human rights in a firm and steadfast manner.

Thank you, Mr. Chairman and distinguished participants, for your attention.

Abd al-Aziz ibn Abd ar-Rahman Al Saud (Ibn Saud) (1880–1953)
The founder of modern Saudi Arabia and its first king (1932–1953). Ibn Saud returned to Riyadh in 1902 from exile and reestablished Saudi control of the city, signaling the beginning of a thirty-year struggle to unite the Arabian Peninsula. During the process of consolidation Ibn Saud also renewed his family's historical alliance with the descendants of Muhammad ibn Abd al-Wahhab. The power-sharing relationship between Wahhabi religious leaders and Saudi political leaders continues to be a defining characteristic of Saudi politics and society. At times this has been a source of tension within the kingdom.

Abd al-Aziz Muhammad Ibn Saud (b.?–1765) A small landowner and broker who founded the settlement of Dir'iyya in the central Arabian province of Najd. His political and military skills earned him the respect of the local population, which allowed him to acquire the title of amir of Dir'iyya in 1727. In 1744 Muhammad ibn Saud formed an alliance with Shaykh Muhammad ibn Abd al-Wahhab and began a campaign to spread the Al Saud family's control, and Wahhab's religious doctrines, across the entire Arabian Peninsula. Muhammad ibn Saud was the first Saudi monarch of any kind, and his alliance with the shaykh continues to be an historical and religious justification of Saudi political authority on the Arabian Peninsula.

Abd al-Rahman ibn Faisal Al Saud (1850–1928) The father of Ibn Saud and the last Saudi amir of Riyadh (1889–1891) until the reestablishment of Saudi authority in 1903. Abd al-Rahman fled with his family to Kuwait in 1893 and formed an alliance with several other local amirs. Together they conducted a series of successful raids against the al Rashid dynasty. These raids against the Rashidi forces, who were in control of Riyadh during the exile of Abd al-Rahman, created the foundation from which Ibn Saud reestablished Saudi control of the city and, eventually, of the modern kingdom of Saudi Arabia.

Abdullah Ibn Abdul Aziz Al Saud (1924–present) Appointed second deputy prime minister following the assassination of King Faisal in 1975. Following the death of King Khalid in 1982, he was appointed deputy prime minister and crown prince. He has also been head of the Saudi National Guard since 1962, transforming and expanding the military's role in Saudi society. After his brother, King Fahd, suffered a stroke in 1995, Abdullah effectively became the head of state in Saudi Arabia. As such, he presided over a significant shift in Saudi foreign policy with the United States and Saudi Arabia's neighbors in the Middle East. Abdullah both distanced himself from the policies of the United States and took a more active role in addressing the dispute between Israel and the Palestinians after the terrorist attacks of September 11, 2001, in New York and Washington, D.C.

Fahd bin Abdul Aziz Al Saud (1923–present) Appointed deputy prime minister and crown prince in 1975 after the death of King Faisal. Fahd became king in 1982 and inherited significant tensions among conservative groups that wanted to protect the Islamic traditions of Saudi Arabia and those groups that wanted to embrace modern technologies and educational techniques. Fahd balanced these concerns by encouraging investment in new technologies while reemphasizing his government's commitment to Islamic causes in the Middle East and south Asia. In 1990 King Fahd invited foreign military forces, led by the United States, to contain and repel the Iraqi invasion of Kuwait. His decision contributed to an increase in opposition to the Al Saud monarchy from conservative religious groups that felt Fahd compromised the kingdom's commitment to Islamic principles by relying on foreign soldiers.

Faisal bin Abdul Aziz Al Saud (1906–1975) Faisal was an important part of his father's efforts to unite the Arabian Peninsula in the 1920s, acting as viceroy of the Hijaz in the years leading up to the establishment of the kingdom in 1932. He served as prime minister under Ibn Saud and became king (1964–1975) after settling a dispute with his half brother Saud. Faisal initiated the full-scale development of the Saudi oil industry and oversaw the economic boom of the late 1960s and the early 1970s, while strengthening his government's commitment to Islamic education in Saudi Arabia. Faisal's policies both placed Saudi Arabia at the center of the Israeli-Palestinian conflict and established Saudi Arabia as one of the most powerful countries in the Middle East—capable of wielding significant influence with Western countries by virtue of its oil wealth.

Juhay ibn Muhammad al Utaybi Born in the Ikhwan settlement of

Sajir in the city of Qasim during the 1920s, al Utaybi was an Islamic preacher who was heavily influenced by the Egyptian Muslim Brotherhood, a conservative Islamic group that gained strength in Saudi Arabia during the reign of King Faisal (1964–1975). Al Utaybi led the siege on the sacred mosque at Mecca in 1979 that spurred a conservative Islamic revival in Saudi Arabia during the 1980s. Historians and scholars consider the siege to be one of the most important manifestations of Islamic fundamentalism in Saudi Arabia. It also served as an indication of the degree to which conservative Muslim groups began to challenge the Al Saud family's relationship with the United States in the final decades of the twentieth century.

Khalid bin Abdul Aziz Al Saud (1913–1982) Khalid served as the governor of Hijaz (1932–1934) and minister of the interior (1934–1975) before becoming king upon the death of Faisal in 1975. Khalid was faced with several pressing developments in regional affairs, especially the emergence of a hostile Shiite regime in Iran following the Iranian revolution of 1979 and with a surge in oppositionist movements inside Saudi Arabia. His reign was also marred by the occupation of the sacred mosque in Mecca in 1979 and the Shia riots of 1980—two of the most notable and open expressions of opposition to the Saudi monarchy in its history. Khalid died in 1982 following a short illness related to a heart condition and was replaced by his brother Fahd, who was already functioning as head of state at the time of Khalid's death.

Muhammad ibn Abd al-Wahhab (1703–1791) Founder of the Wahhabi religious movement, which sought to restore the purity of Islam on the Arabian Peninsula during the eighteenth century. Wahhab's conservative doctrines gained many followers during his lifetime and after his death, aided by the political and military alliance he and his descendants made with the Al Saud family. Wahhab's influence on Saudi society remains strong, and Saudi political leaders still must balance their own authority with that of the Wahhabi religious establishment in order to maintain control of the kingdom.

Osama bin Laden (1957–present) One of approximately fifty children in a wealthy Saudi family that earned its fortune in the construction business. Like many young Saudis at the time, bin Laden joined the Afghan resistance during the war against the Soviets (1979–1989) and returned to Saudi Arabia radicalized by his experience in Afghanistan. After the Gulf War of 1991, bin Laden became a devoted opponent of the Al Saud monarchy and cofounded al-Qaeda, one of the world's most notorious international terrorist groups.

Saud bin Abdul Aziz Al Saud (1902–1969) Became the second king of Saudi Arabia (1953–1964) after the death of Ibn Saud in 1953. Saud was involved in a dispute with his brother Faisal over the future of the kingdom almost immediately after ascending the throne vacated by his father. Ultimately, he was removed on charges of mismanagement of the economy. He was replaced by Faisal after a power struggle between competing factions within the royal family.

Talal ibn Abd al-Aziz (1931–present) A minor prince in the Saudi royal family who became the minister of finance (1960–1962) during a quarrel between King Saud and his brother, Crown Prince Faisal. Talal is known for leading a liberal opposition movement called the "free princes," which hoped to reform the Saudi government by creating a freely elected assembly to check the power of the Saudi monarch. The movement was one of the most notable expressions of dissent in Saudi Arabia and signaled potentially destabilizing rifts within the royal family. Talal was exiled to Egypt in 1962 and continues to be a strong critic of the Saudi monarchy.

Turki ibn Abdallah ibn Muhammad ibn Saud (b.?–1834) Turki restored Saudi authority in the area around Riyadh after the Egyptian invasion of 1811; he ruled there from 1823 until his death in 1834. Turki is the grandfather of Ibn Saud, the founder of modern Saudi Arabia, and the founder of the second Saudi state (which held authority in Riyadh until the 1890s). He was the first of the contemporary line of Saudi monarchs, and in many ways he was responsible for maintaining a foothold for Saudi political authority on the Arabian Peninsula in the nineteenth century.

🔥 GLOSSARY

bedouins: Nomadic Arabs that traditionally made their living breeding camels and sheep in the desert interior of Arabia. Bedouins represent roughly 10 percent of the total population in the Middle East and continue to make up a large portion of the Saudi population in the twenty-first century.

bid'a: Religious innovation or heresy. In the eighteenth century Wahhabi clerics fought rigorously to remove religious innovation from the practices of Muslims in Arabia and emphasized a literal interpretation of the Koran.

caliph (kalifah): A word referring to the earthly ruler of the entire Muslim community (the *ummah*). After Muhammad's death in 632 B.C., a conflict over who should rightfully be named caliph emerged within the Islamic religion. This disagreement produced Islam's two major branches, the Sunnis and the Shiites.

emir (amir): Arabic word meaning ruler or prince. Areas under the authority of an amir in the Arab world are known as emirates.

fatwa: A religious opinion, or ruling, issued by an expert in Islamic law (*shariah*). Islamic scholars regularly issue fatwas in order to communicate their interpretations of current events, technological changes, and public policies to Muslims around the world.

hadith: The teachings of the prophet Muhammad through his words and deeds, as well as his interpretations of the behavior of individuals in his presence. There are currently two major collections of the hadith; these are based on the Sunni / Shiite division within the Islamic religion.

hajj: The Arabic word for pilgrimage. Every year millions of Muslims from all over the world make the yearly hajj to Mecca. This trip is required of each Muslim at least once in his or her life. The hajj corresponds with the Islamic holy day *id al-adha*, which commemorates Abraham's willingness to sacrifice his son to God.

haram: In Islamic theology, a word meaning sanctuary or sacred territory. The Saudi cities Mecca and Medina are examples of *haram*, as they are the two most sacred sites in the Islamic religion.

Ikhwan: An Arabic word that means Muslim brothers or companions. In Saudi history the Ikhwan were a tribal military force that professed loyalty to Ibn Saud with the conditions that he recognize the religious authority of Wahhabi clerics and that he remain committed to their interpretation of Islamic law.

imam: A word that, among Shiite Muslims, refers to a teacher of Islam. To many Muslims in the Sunni tradition, imam has become synonymous with caliph, which refers to a title once reserved for the earthly ruler of Muslims.

intifada: An Arabic word that literally means awakening from sleep. In contemporary usage *intifada* refers to Palestinian uprisings against the Israeli occupation of the West Bank and Gaza Strip in the late twentieth and early twenty-first centuries.

jihad: The term literally refers to an individual Muslim's internal struggle against evil, but it also refers to a struggle against heretical beliefs and practices in general. In contemporary usage the most common translation for jihad is holy war.

Kuffar (Kufr): A word that literally means refusal to submit to the will of Allah, or disbelief in Islam. *Kuffar* is often used interchangeably as an adjective or a noun. It can refer to non-Islamic policies, laws, or people (heretics).

majlis: A public council or assembly. The *majlis* is a traditional institution in Arabian society. Disputes were settled between important Arab leaders at these public meetings. During the early years of the modern Saudi state, Ibn Saud used the *majlis* to display his power. But after the first few decades of his rule, the institution waned in importance.

mullah: A title of respect for those with substantial training in Islamic theocracy and law in the Persian-speaking world. Generally, a mullah also teaches young Muslim students in schools with religious curricula called *madrassahs.*

mutawaa'in (**sing.** *mutawwa*): Religious specialists, or volunteers, from the Arabian province of Najd. During Ibn Saud's campaign to unite the Arabian Peninsula, the *mutawaa'in* proved extremely important for its success. In contemporary Saudi Arabia the *mutawaa'in* are responsible for enforcing laws governing public morality, including those that regulate the dress and movement of Saudi women in public places.

Ottoman Empire: A Turkish empire that ruled much of the Middle East and portions of south Asia from the fourteenth century to the early twentieth century. Nominally, the Ottoman Empire controlled the territory of modern Saudi Arabia until the end of World War I, but much of the interior remained relatively independent in spite of superior Turkish military power.

qadi: An Arabic world meaning religious judge. Muhammad ibn Abd al-Wahhab's father was a *qadi*, and Wahhab himself received training in Islamic jurisprudence before devoting himself to the purification of Islam on the Arabian Peninsula in the eighteenth century.

shariah: The law of Islam. *Shariah* is based on a four-tiered foundation: the Koran, hadith (the teachings of Muhammad), the consensus of Muslims, and reasoning by analogy. Reasoning by analogy allows Islamic judges, or *qadi*, to interpret circumstances that are not explicitly covered by the Koran or hadith.

shaykh: A religious title of honor in the Islamic religion. The title is usually reserved for Muslims who exhibit qualities of one who is in direct contact with God. In the English-speaking world, this title most commonly refers to Muslims who are believed to be mystics.

Shia Islam: The second largest branch of Islam, composed of 10 to 15 percent of all Muslims. Shia Islam developed in the seventh century as a result of a dispute with Sunni Muslims over principles of succession after the death of Muhammad. Followers of Shia Islam (Shiites) recognized Muhammad's son-in-law, Ali, as the first legitimate caliph, while Sunnis recognized Abu Bakr.

Sufi (Sufism): A strand of Islamic thought that emphasizes a continuous path to God in daily life. Sufism places much less emphasis on the notion of an afterlife than do orthodox Sunnis and

Shiites, and it rejects the notions of heavenly reward and divine punishment as motivations for pious behavior.

Sunni Islam: The largest branch of Islam, consisting of 85 to 90 percent of all Muslims. Sunnis recognized Abu Bakr as the first legitimate caliph after the death of Muhammad, and they typically settled issues of succession through consensus thereafter. Sunni Islam is also the aggregate of four major traditions in Islamic jurisprudence: the Hanafi, Maliki, Shafii, and Hanbali schools.

tawhid: A religious doctrine that is especially important in the Wahhabi tradition. *Tawhid* stresses the unity of God and requires Muslims to deny all idols and all other deities in their religious observances.

ulama (sing. alim): Religious scholars who have received special training in Islamic law and theology. In Saudi Arabia, Wahhabi ulema played an important role in Ibn Saud's conquest of the Arabian Peninsula and remains an important component of Saudi political authority.

ummah: Literally translates to mean the community. In the Islamic tradition, *ummah* simply refers to all Muslims.

Wahhabi (Wahhabism): A conservative strand of Islamic thought and jurisprudence named for its founder, Muhammad ibn Abd Al-Wahhab. Wahhabism originated in eighteenth-century Arabia and continues to be the official religion of Saudi Arabia in the twenty-first century.

zakat: A religious tax paid to Arabian imams, or kings. After his alliance with Muhammad ibn Abd Al-Wahhab, Muhammad Ibn Saud received this tax and used it, in part, to extend his political control beyond the small desert oasis of Dir'iyya in central Arabia.

🔥 CHRONOLOGY

1000 B.C.
Minean kingdom flourishing in southwestern Arabia.

100 B.C.
Nabatean kingdom established in the north of the Arabian Peninsula.

A.D. 400s
Mecca becomes the leading city of Arabia.

570
Birth of Muhammad.

622
Muhammad and a band of followers flee Mecca and migrate to Medina.

630
Muhammad captures Mecca, marking the beginning of a period of expansion leading to the Islamic empire.

1400s
Saud dynasty founded in the region around modern Riyadh.

1517
Control of most of the Arabian Peninsula passes to the Ottomans.

ca. 1750
Wahhabi movement begins in Najd in the center of Arabia.

1802
Mecca is conquered by the Wahhabis.

1812
Wahhabis are driven out of Mecca.

1818
Wahhabis and Sauds join to establish their capital at Riyadh.

1865
Sauds lose control of Riyadh and their realm is divided between different clans and the Ottomans.

1891
The Al Saud family exiled to Kuwait.

1902
Ibn Saud retakes Riyadh.

1906
Saud forces regain control over Najd.

1924
Ibn Saud takes Mecca without bloodshed.

1925
Ibn Saud takes Medina.

1926
Ibn Saud declares himself king of Hijaz.

1928–1930
The Ikhwan turn against Ibn Saud but are defeated.

1932
Ibn Saud unifies the conquered territories and names the new country Saudi Arabia.

1938
Oil is discovered in the eastern provinces.

1939
Oil production begins under the U.S.-controlled Aramco (Arabian American Oil Company); Ibn Saud initiates large-scale modernization.

1940–1945
Saudi Arabia allows the United States to establish an air base at Dharan during World War II.

1951
An agreement with Aramco gives Saudi Arabia 50 percent of all earnings from oil.

1953
King Ibn Saud dies; he is succeeded by his son Saud.

1960
Saudi Arabia helps establish OPEC to help sustain international oil prices.

1962
King Saud transfers power to his brother Faisal; relations with Egypt are severed over Egypt's role in Yemen-based revolution.

1964
Prince Faisal officially replaces Saud as king.

1967
Saudi Arabia sends twenty thousand soldiers to fight in the Arab-Israeli Six Day War; Saudi Arabia normalizes relations with Egypt.

1973
Saudi Arabia plays a leading role in an oil boycott against Western countries that support Israel; world oil prices skyrocket.

1975
King Faisal is assassinated.

1979
Saudi Arabia severs diplomatic relations with Egypt after Egypt makes peace with Israel; a group of Sunni Muslims barricade themselves inside the Great Mosque in Mecca, forcing the Saudi army to retake the mosque with great loss of life.

1980
Saudi Arabia takes control of Aramco.

1982
King Khalid dies; he is succeeded by Fahd.

1987
Saudi Arabia resumes diplomatic relations with Egypt; four hundred Iranian pilgrims are killed after clashes with Saudi security forces in Mecca.

1990
Iraq invades Kuwait; Saudi Arabia invites hundreds of thousands of

foreign troops (mainly from the United States) to use Saudi Arabia as a base.

1991
Saudi Arabia is involved in air attacks on Iraq and in the land force that went on to liberate Kuwait.

1992
King Fahd proposes steps toward greater political expression in the kingdom.

1993
Saudi Arabia experiences severe budget deficits, mainly as a result of the Persian Gulf War.

1994
270 people die in Mecca during a stampede, raising international criticism of Saudi Arabia's ability to protect pilgrims.

1995
King Fahd has a stroke and the job of running the country falls mainly to Crown Prince Abdullah.

1996
King Fahd resumes control of state affairs; a bomb explodes at a U.S. military complex near Dharan killing nineteen and wounding more than three hundred.

1999
For the first time, Saudi women attend the meeting of an official organization looking into expanding political expression in the kingdom.

2000
September: The London-based human rights group Amnesty International issues a report condemning the treatment of women and foreign domestic workers in Saudi Arabia.

2001
April: Saudi Arabia and Iran take major steps toward normalizing their relations by signing an agreement to combat terrorism, drug trafficking, and organized crime in the Middle East.
May: The United Nations Committee Against Torture issues a state-

ment criticizing Saudi Arabia for violating international conventions against cruel and unusual punishment.

September: Saudi Arabia breaks diplomatic ties with the Taliban in Afghanistan after the Taliban leadership refuses to turn over Osama bin Laden, the prime suspect in the September 11 terrorist attacks, to international authorities.

December: Saudi king Fahd condemns the September 11 terrorist attacks on New York and Washington, D.C., and calls for an international campaign to eradicate terrorism.

2002

February: Crown Prince Abdullah discloses his plan for peace between the Israelis and the Palestinians, calling for Arab recognition of Israel in exchange for an autonomous Palestinian state.

June: Saudi authorities arrest eleven Saudis, a Sudanese, and an Iraqi with suspected links to the al-Qaeda terrorist network after uncovering their plans to attack key military targets in Saudi Arabia with explosives and surface-to-air missiles.

October: Saudi Arabia and Iraq take steps toward reestablishing diplomatic relations by opening a border crossing between the two countries for the first time since Iraq's invasion of Kuwait in 1990.

November: The Saudi government announces it will not allow the United States to use its facilities in the Persian Gulf to attack Iraq, even if the action were sanctioned by the United Nations.

2003

January: A group of prominent Saudi liberals and Islamists petition Crown Prince Abdullah, calling for the introduction of elections, eradication of corruption, and economic reform in order to promote more popular control of the Saudi government. It was the first time in the history of Saudi Arabia that the Saudi monarch received such a petition without jailing the petitioners.

◆ FOR FURTHER RESEARCH

Books

Said K. Aburish, *The Rise, Corruption, and Coming Fall of the House of Saud.* London: Bloomsbury, 1994.

Haifa Alangari, *The Struggle for Power in Arabia: Ibn Saud, Hussein, and Great Britain, 1914–1924.* Reading, England: Ithaca Press, 1998.

Mona AlMunajjed, *Women in Saudi Arabia Today.* New York: St. Martin's Press, 1997.

Frederick Fallowfield Anscombe, *The Ottoman Gulf: The Creation of Kuwait, Saudi Arabia, and Qatar.* New York: Columbia University Press, 1997.

Mamoun Fandy, *Saudi Arabia and the Politics of Dissent.* New York: St. Martin's Press, 1999.

John S. Habib, *Ibn Sa'ud's Warriors of Islam: The Ikhwan of Najd and Their Role in the Creation of the Sa'udi Kingdom, 1910–1930.* Leiden, the Netherlands: E.J. Brill, 1978.

Robert G. Hoyland, *Arabia and the Arabs: From the Bronze Age to the Coming of Islam.* New York: Routledge, 2001.

Sheikh Mohammad Iqbal, *Emergence of Saudi Arabia: A Political Study of King Abd al-Aziz ibn Saud, 1901–1953.* Srinagar, India: Saudiyah, 1977.

Sarah Izraeli, *The Remaking of Saudi Arabia: The Struggle Between King Sa'ud and Crown Prince Faysal, 1953–1962.* Tel Aviv, Israel: Moshe Dayan Center for Middle Eastern and African Studies, Tel Aviv University, 1997.

Anders Jerichow, *Saudi Arabia: Outside Global Law and Order, a Discussion Paper.* Richmond, England: Curzon Press, 1997.

John Peterson, *Saudi Arabia and the Illusion of Security.* London: Oxford University Press, for the International Institute for Strategic Studies, 2002.

Madawi Al-Rasheed, *A History of Saudi Arabia*. New York: Cambridge University Press, 2002.

Nasser Ibrahim Rashid and Esber Ibrahim Shaheen, *Saudi Arabia and the Gulf War*. Joplin, MO: International Institute of Technology, 1992.

Gary Troeller, *The Birth of Saudi Arabia: Britain and the Rise of the House of Sa'ud*. London: F. Cass, 1976.

Aleksei Mikhailovich Vasilev, *The History of Saudi Arabia*. London: Saqi Books, 1998.

Mai Yamani, *Changed Identities: The Challenge of the New Generation in Saudi Arabia*. London: Royal Institute of International Affairs; Washington, DC: Distributed by the Brookings Institution, 2000.

Ayman Al-Yassini, *Religion and State in the Kingdom of Saudi Arabia*. Boulder, CO: Westview Press, 1985.

Periodicals

Youssef H. Aboul-Enein, "The Monarch and His Army: An Examination of Power Relations in Saudi Arabia," *Marine Corps Gazette*, vol. 81, no. 8, August 1997, pp. 42–44.

Lisa Beyer, "The Women of Islam," *Time*, vol. 158, no. 24, December 3, 2001, pp. 50–56.

Milton R. Copulos, "Q: Should the United States Shut Down Its Military Bases in Saudi Arabia?" *Insight on the News*, vol. 18, no. 15, April 29, 2002, pp. 40–43.

R. Hrair Dekmejian, "Saudi Arabia's Consultative Council," *Middle East Journal*, vol. 52, no. 2, Spring 1998, pp. 204–19.

Brian Duffy, "Bombs in the Desert," *U.S. News & World Report*, vol. 121, no. 2, July 8, 1996, pp. 28–33.

Mamoun Fandy et al., "The Abdulla Peace Plan: Offer or Ultimatum?" *Middle East Policy*, vol. 9, no. 3, September 2002, pp. 1–21.

Neil Ford, "Saudi Arabia Moves Towards Diversification," *Middle East*, September 2002, pp. 27–37.

Nathan Gardels, "Saudi Arabia's Wahhabis Are Not Spreading Intolerance," *New Perspectives Quarterly*, vol. 19, no. 2, Spring 2002, pp. 65–70.

Gregory F. Gause III, "Be Careful What You Wish For: The Future of U.S.-Saudi Relations," *World Policy Journal*, vol. 19, no. 1, Spring 2002, pp. 37–51.

Tony Hays, "House of Saud: A House of Sand," *Insight on the News*, vol. 17, no. 48, December 24, 2001, pp. 22–25.

Dilip Hiro, "Saudi 'Reforms': Too Little and Thirty-Two Years Late," *Nation*, vol. 254, no. 14, April 13, 1992, pp. 484–87.

Bernard Lewis, "License to Kill: Usama bin Ladin's Declaration of Jihad," *Foreign Affairs*, vol. 77, no. 6, November/December, 1998, pp. 14–20.

Deroy Murdock, "Is Regime Change in Order for Erstwhile Ally Saudi Arabia?" *Insight on the News*, vol. 18, no. 33, September 9, 2002, p. 46.

Joseph Nevo, "Religion and National Identity in Saudi Arabia," *Middle Eastern Studies*, vol. 34, no. 3, July 1998, pp. 34–44.

Nawaf E. Obaid, "In Al-Saud We Trust," *Foreign Policy*, January/February 2002, pp. 72–74.

Gwenn Okruhlik, "Networks of Dissent: Islamism and Reform in Saudi Arabia," *Current History*, vol. 101, no. 651, January 2002, pp. 22–28.

Amitabh Pal, "The Royal Treatment," *Progressive*, vol. 66, no. 9, September 2002, pp. 27–30.

Martin Peretz, "Veiled Threat," *New Republic*, vol. 226, no. 3, January 28, 2002, pp. 12–14.

Madawi Al-Rasheed, "God, the King, and the Nation: Political Rhetoric in Saudi Arabia in the 1990s," *Middle East Journal*, vol. 50, no. 3, Summer 1996, pp. 359–72.

———, "The Shi'a of Saudi Arabia: A Minority in Search of Cultural Authenticity," *British Journal of Middle Eastern Studies*, vol. 25, no. 1, May 1998, pp. 121–39.

Madawi Al-Rasheed and Loulouwa Al-Rasheed, "The Politics of Encapsulation: Saudi Policy Towards Tribal and Religious Opposition," *Middle Eastern Studies*, vol. 32, no. 1, January 1996, pp. 96–120.

William A. Rugh, "Education in Saudi Arabia: Choices and Constraints," *Middle East Policy*, vol. 9, no. 2, June 2002, pp. 40–56.

Stephen Schwartz, "And the Bandar Played On," *Weekly Standard*, vol. 7, no. 48, September 9, 2002, pp. 18–21.

Jean-Francois Seznec, "Stirrings in Saudi Arabia," *Journal of Democracy*, vol. 13, no. 4, October 2002, 33–40.

Websites

Arab View: The Internet Home of Independent Arab Opinions, www.arabview.com. This site offers access to hundreds of opinion pieces written by Arab journalists from around the world on contemporary issues of importance to Arabs and Muslims. The contributors to this site are also professional journalists from Saudi Arabia and other countries in the Middle East and Europe.

Royal Embassy of Saudi Arabia, www.saudiembassy.net. This site provides general information on the history and culture of Saudi Arabia and access to press releases from important Saudi politicians and ambassadors. There are also links to travel guides and other information, including links to the online publications *Saudi Arabia: The Magazine* and *Saudi Arabia: The Newsletter.*

Saudi Arabia: A Country Study, http://memory.loc.gov. This site offers a comprehensive overview of Saudi history, society, politics, and government, as well as an enormous amount of demographic and economic data about Saudi Arabia up to 1992. Selections include an overview of pre-Islamic history on the Arabian Peninsula and a broad overview of Saudi history since 1932.

Saudi Arabian Information Resource, www.saudinf.com. This site offers a wide array of information on Saudi Arabian history and politics, as well as a wealth of current demographic and economic data. In addition, there is a news link that provides access to current affairs in Saudi Arabia through the lens of the official Saudi press.

♨ INDEX